Dedication

This book is dedicated to my wife, Dori. Without her unending support, tireless editorial efforts, thoughtful criticisms, and patience, I could not have finished my work. Thank you, Dori.

Acknowledgments

My collaborator and co-teacher for eight years, Dennis Kretschman, deserves special mention at this juncture. Together we developed the activities, projects, and courses that became a "learning to learn" curriculum. Dennis designed and taught several of the projects described in these pages, and he added constantly to the spirit and excitement of an independent learning philosophy that gradually evolved into this set of five books. I deeply appreciate the contribution Dennis has made to my work.

I would also like to thank the following people for their advice, support, and advocacy: J. Q. Adams; Dr. Robert Barr; Robert Cole, Jr.; Mary Dalheim; Dr. John Feldhusen; David Humphrey; Bruce Ottenweller; Dr. William Parrett; Ed Saunders; Charles Whaley; and a special thanks to all the kids who have attended John Ball Zoo School since I started working on this project: 1973–1985.

About the Author

PHIL SCHLEMMER, M.Ed., has been creating and teaching independent learning projects since 1973, when he began his master's program in alternative education at Indiana University. Assigned to Grand Rapids, Michigan, for his internship, he helped develop a full-time school for 52 motivated sixth graders. The school was located at the city zoo and immediately became known as the "Zoo School." This program became an experimental site where he remained through the 1984–85 school year, with one year out as director of a high school independent study program.

Presently working as a private consultant, Mr. Schlemmer has been presenting in-services and workshops to teachers, parents, administrators, and students for more than 13 years and has published articles in *Phi Delta Kappan* and *Instructor.*

Social Studies Projects

Phil Schlemmer

Illustrated by Patricia A. Sussman

LEARNING ON YOUR OWN!

Individual, Group, and Classroom
Research Projects for
Gifted and Motivated Students

THE CENTER FOR APPLIED
RESEARCH IN EDUCATION

Library of Congress Cataloging-in-Publication Data

Schlemmer, Phillip L.
    Social studies projects.
    (Learning on your own: unit 5)
    ISBN 0-87628-510-8
    1. Social sciences—Study and teaching (Elementary)—
United States.   2. Project method in teaching.
3. Independent study.   4. Gifted children—Education
(Elementary)—United States. I. Title. II. Series:
Schlemmer, Phillip L.   Learning on your own!; unit 5.
LB1584.S365   1987   86-23250
372.8'3044   CIP

Printed in the United States of America

10 9 8

ISBN 0-87628-510-8

**THE CENTER FOR APPLIED RESEARCH
IN EDUCATION**
West Nyack, NY 10994

On the World Wide Web at http://www.phdirect.com

Foreword

This series of books will become invaluable aids in programs for motivated, gifted, and talented children. They provide clear guidelines and procedures for involving these children in significant learning experiences in research and high level thinking skills while not neglecting challenging learning within the respective basic disciplines of science, mathematics, social studies, and writing. The approach is one that engages the interests of children at a deep level. I have seen Phil Schlemmer at work teaching with the materials and methods presented in these books and have been highly impressed with the quality of learning which was taking place. While I recognized Phil is an excellent teacher, it nevertheless seemed clear that the method and the materials were making a strong and significant contribution to the children's learning.

Children will learn how to carry out research and will become independent lifelong learners through the skills acquired from the program of studies presented in these books. Success in independent study and research and effective use of libraries and other information resources are not simply products of trial-and-error activity in school. They are products of teacher guidance and stimulation along with instructional materials and methods and an overall system which provides the requisite skills and attitudes.

All of the material presented in this series of books has undergone extensive tryout. The author has also spent thousands of hours developing, writing, revising, and editing, but above all he has spent his time conceptualizing and designing a dynamic system for educating motivated, gifted, and talented youth. The net result is a program of studies which should make an invaluable contribution to the education of these youth. And, above all that, I am sure that if it is taught well, the kids will love it.

John F. Feldhusen, Ph.D., Director
Gifted Education Resource Institute
Purdue University
West Lafayette, Indiana 47907

About Learning on Your Own!

In the summer of 1973, I was offered the opportunity of a lifetime. The school board in Grand Rapids, Michigan authorized a full-time experimental program for 52 motivated sixth-grade children, and I was asked to help start it. The school was described as an environmental studies program, and its home was established in two doublewide house trailers that were connected and converted into classrooms. This building was placed in the parking lot of Grand Rapids' municipal zoo (John Ball Zoological Gardens). Naturally, the school came to be known as "The Zoo School."

The mandate for the Zoo School staff was clear—to build a challenging, stimulating, and interesting curriculum that was in no way limited by the school system's stated sixth-grade objectives. Operating with virtually no textbooks or "regular" instructional materials, we had the freedom to develop our own projects and courses, schedule our own activities, and design our own curriculum.

Over a period of ten years, hundreds of activities were created to use with motivated learners. This was a golden opportunity because few teachers are given a chance to experiment with curriculum in an isolated setting with the blessing of the school board. When a project worked, I wrote about it, recorded the procedures that were successful, filed the handouts, and organized the materials so that someone else could teach it. The accumulation of projects for motivated children led to a book proposal which, in turn, led to this five-book series. *Learning on Your Own!* is based entirely on actual classroom experience. Every project and activity has been used successfully with children in the areas of

- Research Skills
- Writing
- Science
- Mathematics
- Social Studies

As the books evolved and materialized over the years, it seemed that they would be useful to classroom teachers, especially in the upper elementary and junior high grades. This became increasingly clear as teachers from a wide variety of settings were presented with ideas from the books. Teachers saw different uses for the projects, based upon the abilities of their students and their own curricular needs.

Learning on Your Own! will be useful to you for any of the following reasons:

- If a curricular goal is to teach children to be independent learners, then skill development is necessary. The projects in each book are arranged according to the level of independence that is required—the early projects can be used to *teach* skills; the later ones require their *use*.

- These projects prepare the way for students confidently to make use of higher-level thinking skills.

- A broad range of students can benefit from projects that are skill-oriented. They need not be gifted/talented.

- On the other hand, teachers of the gifted/talented will see that the emphasis on independence and higher-level thinking makes the projects fit smoothly into their curricular goals.

- The projects are designed for use by one teacher with a class of up to 30 students. They are intentionally built to accommodate the "regular" class-room teacher. Projects that require 1-to-1 or even 1-to-15 teacher-student ratios are of little use to most teachers.

- The books do not represent a curriculum that must be followed. Gifted/talented programs may have curricula based upon the five-book series, and individual situations may allow for the development of a "learning to learn" curriculum. Generally speaking, however, each project is self-contained and need not be a part of a year-long progression of courses and projects.

- Each project offers a format that can be used even if the *content* is changed. You may, with some modification, apply many projects toward subject material that is already being taught. This provides a means of delivering the same message in a different way.

- Most teachers have students in their classes capable of pursuing projects that are beyond the scope of the class as a whole. These books can be used to provide special projects for such students so that they may learn on their own.

- One of the most pervasive concepts in *Learning on Your Own!* is termed "kids teaching kids." Because of the emphasis placed on students teaching one another, oral presentations are required for many projects. This reinforces the important idea that not only can students *learn*, they can also *teach*. Emphasis on oral presentation can be reduced if time constraints demand it.

- The premise of this series is that children, particularly those who are motivated to learn, need a base from which to expand their educational horizons. Specifically, this base consists of five important components of independent learning:

—skills

—confidence

—a mandate to pursue independence

—projects that show students *how* to learn on their own

—an opportunity to practice independent learning

Learning on Your Own! places primary emphasis on the motivated learner, the definition of which is left intentionally ambiguous. It is meant to include most normal children who have natural curiosities and who understand the need for a good education. Motivated children are important people who deserve recognition for their ability and desire to achieve. The trend toward understanding the special needs and incredible potential of children who enjoy the adventure and challenge of learning is encouraging. Teachers, parents, business people, community leaders, and concerned citizens are beginning to seriously ask, "What can we do for these young people who want to learn?"

Creating a special program or developing a new curriculum is not necessarily the answer. Many of the needs of these children can be met in the regular classroom by teaching basic independent learning skills. No teacher can possibly master and teach all of the areas that his or her students may be interested in studying, but every teacher has opportunities to place emphasis on basic learning skills. A surprising number of children become more motivated as they gain skills that allow them to learn independently. "Learning on your own" is an important concept because it, in itself, provides motivation. You can contribute to your students' motivation by emphasizing self-confidence and skill development. One simple project during a semester can give students insight into the usefulness of independent learning. One lesson that emphasizes a skill can bring students a step closer to choosing topics, finding information, planning projects, and making final presentations without assistance. By teaching motivated students *how to learn on their own,* you give them the ability to challenge themselves, to transcend the six-hour school day.

Beyond meeting the immediate needs of individual students, teaching children how to learn on their own will have an impact on their adult lives and may affect society itself. It is easy to discuss the day-to-day importance of independent learning in one breath, and in the next be talking of the needs of adults 30 years from now. This five-book series is based upon the assumption that educating children to be independent learners makes sense in a complicated, rapidly changing, unpredictable world. Preparing today's children for tomorrow's challenges is of paramount importance to educators and parents, but a monumental task lies in deciding what can be taught that will have lasting value in years to come. What will people need to know in the year 2001 and beyond? Can we accurately prescribe a set of facts and information that will be *necessary* to an average citizen 10, 20, or 30 years from now? Can we feel confident that what we teach will be useful, or even relevant, by the time our students become adults? Teaching children to be independent learners is a compelling response to these difficult, thought-provoking questions.

How to Use
Learning on Your Own!

Learning on Your Own! can be used in many ways. The projects and the overall design of the books lend themselves to a variety of applications, such as basic skill activities, full-class units or courses, small-group projects, independent study, and even curriculum development. Regardless of how the series is to be implemented, it is important to understand its organization and recognize what it provides. Like a good cookbook, this series supplies more than a list of ingredients. It offers suggestions, advice, and hints; provides organization and structure; and gives time-lines, handouts, and materials lists. In other words, it supplies everything necessary for you to conduct the projects.

These books were produced with you in mind. Every project is divided into three general sections to provide uniformity throughout the series and to give each component a standard placement in the material. The first section, Teacher Preview, gives a brief overview of the scope and focus of the project. The second section, Lesson Plans and Notes, outlines a detailed, hour-by-hour description. After reading this, every nuance of the project should be understood. The third section, Instructional Materials, supplies the "nuts-and-bolts" of the project—reproducible assignment sheets, instructional handouts, tests, answer sheets, and evaluations.

Here is a concise explanation of each of the three sections. Read this material before going further to better understand how the projects can be used.

Teacher Preview

The Teacher Preview is a quick explanation of what a project accomplishes or teaches. It is divided into seven areas, each of which provides specific information about the project:

Length of Project: The length of each project is given in classroom hours. It does not take into account homework or teacher-preparation time.

Level of Independence: Each project is identified as "basic," "intermediate," or "advanced" in terms of how much independence is required of students. The level of independence is based primarily on how many decisions a student must make and how much responsibility is required. It is suggested that students who have not acquired independent learning skills, regardless of their grade level, be carefully introduced to advanced projects.

For teachers who are interested, there is a correlation between the skill development mentioned here and the progression to higher-level thinking skills typified by Benjamin Bloom's "Taxonomy of Educational Objectives":

Level of Independence	*Bloom's Taxonomy*
Basic	Knowledge
	Comprehension
Intermediate	Application
	Analysis
Advanced	Synthesis
	Evaluation

Goals: These are straightforward statements of what a project is designed to accomplish. Goals that recur throughout the series deal with skill development, independent learning, and "kids teaching kids."

During This Project Students Will: This is a list of concise project objectives. Occasionally, some of these statements become activities rather than objectives, but they are included because they help specify what students will do during the course of a project.

Skills: Each project emphasizes a specific set of skills, which are listed in this section. Further information about the skills is provided in the "Skills Chart." You may change the skill emphasis of a project according to curricular demands or the needs of the students.

Handouts Provided: The handouts provided with a project are listed by name. This includes assignment sheets, informational handouts, tests, and evaluation forms.

Project Calendar: This is a chart that graphically shows each hour of instruction. Since it does not necessarily represent consecutive days, lines are provided for you to pencil in dates. The calendar offers a synopsis of each hour's activity and also brief notes to clue you about things that must be done:

PREPARATION REQUIRED   STUDENTS TURN IN WORK
NEED SPECIAL MATERIALS   RETURN STUDENT WORK
HANDOUT PROVIDED   ANSWER SHEET PROVIDED

Lesson Plans and Notes

The lesson plan is a detailed hour-by-hour description of a project, explaining its organization and presentation methods. Projects can be shortened by reducing the time spent on such things as topic selection, research, and presentation; however, this necessitates de-emphasizing skills that make real independent study possible. Alternately, a project may require additional hours if students are weak in particular skill areas or if certain concepts are not thoroughly understood.

Each hour's lesson plan is accompanied by notes about the project. Some notes are fairly extensive if they are needed to clarify subject matter or describe a process.

Instructional Material

There are five types of reproducible instructional materials included in *Learning on Your Own!* Most projects can be run successfully with just a Student Assignment Sheet; the rest of the materials are to be used as aids at your discretion.

Student Assignment Sheets: Virtually every project has an assignment sheet that explains the project and outlines requirements.

Additional Handouts: Some projects offer other handouts to supply basic information or provide a place to record answers or research data.

Tests and Quizzes: Tests and quizzes are included with projects that present specific content. Since most projects are individualized, the activities themselves are designed to test student comprehension and skill development.

Evaluation Sheets: Many projects provide their own evaluation sheets. In addition, the Teacher's Introduction to the Student Research Guide (see the Appendix) contains evaluations for notecards, posters, and oral presentations. Some projects also supply self-evaluation forms so that students can evaluate their own work.

Forms, Charts, Lists: These aids are provided throughout the series. They are designed for specific situations in individual projects.

OTHER FEATURES OF
LEARNING ON YOUR OWN!

In addition to the projects, each book in the series offers several other useful features:

Grade Level: A grade level notation of upper elementary, junior high, and/or high is shown next to each project in the table of contents. Because this series was developed with gifted/talented/motivated sixth-graders, junior high is the logical grade level for most projects; thus, generally speaking, these projects are most appropriate for students in grades 6–8.

Skills Chart: This is a chart listing specific independent learning skills that may be applied to each project. It is fully explained in its introductory material.

Teacher's Introduction to the Student Research Guide: This introduction is found in the Appendix. It offers suggestions for conducting research projects and provides several evaluation forms.

Student Research Guide: Also found in the Appendix, this is a series of checklists that can be used by students working on individualized projects. The Daily Log, for example, is a means of having students keep track of their own progress. In addition to the checklists, there are instructional handouts on basic research skills.

General Notes

Examine the *structure* of the projects in each book, even if the titles do not fit specific needs. Many projects are so skill-oriented that content can be drastically altered without affecting the goals.

Many projects are dependent upon resource materials; the more sources of information, the better. Some ways of providing materials for the classroom are to

- Ask parents for donations of books and magazines.
- Advertise for specific materials in the classified section of the newspaper.
- Check out library materials for a mini-library in the classroom.
- Gradually purchase useful materials as they are discovered.
- Take trips to public libraries and make use of school libraries.

Students may not initially recognize the value of using notecards. They will soon learn, however, that the cards allow data to be recorded as individual facts that can be arranged and rearranged at will.

"Listening" is included as an important skill in most projects. In lecture situations, class discussions, and when students are giving presentations, you should require students to listen and respect the right of others to listen.

Provide time for grading and returning materials to students during the course of a project. The Project Calendar is convenient for planning a schedule.

A visual display is often a requirement for projects in this series. Students usually choose to make a poster, but there are other possibilities:

mural	collage	demonstration	dramatization
mobile	model	display or exhibit	book, magazine, or pamphlet
diorama	puppet show	slide show	

When students work on their own, your role changes from information supplier to learning facilitator. It is also important to help students solve their own problems so that momentum and forward progress are maintained.

A FINAL NOTE FROM THE AUTHOR

Learning on Your Own! provides the materials and the structure that are necessary for individualized learning. The only missing elements are the enthusiasm, vitality, and creative energy that are needed to ignite a group of students and set them diligently to work on projects that require concentration and perseverance. I hope that *my* work will make *your* work easier by letting you put your efforts into quality and innovation. The ability to learn independently is perhaps the greatest gift that can be conferred upon students. Give it with the knowledge that it is valuable beyond price, uniquely suited to each individual, and good for a lifetime!

Phil Schlemmer

About This Book

Social studies is a field of education so vast that it defies description. There is virtually no end to the number of subjects, topics, and subtopics that could be listed under the heading "Social Studies." For this reason, social studies offers a perfect opportunity to teach children about independent learning. The projects in this book are designed to help students learn on their own; skills are emphasized over content. The goal of each project is to help students choose topics; find, record, and organize information; plan presentations; solve whatever problems arise; and present their work to others.

The first five projects in the book (Who's in the News Bulletin Board, Newspaper Collages, Current Archaeology, The U.S.S.R., and Geography) are full-class projects that require a basic level of independence. They can also be modified for use with small groups or a few individuals. The next two projects (Historical Study and Famous People) are intermediate. They, too, are designed for full-class use, but students work on their own to collect information and design presentations. The remaining projects (Early American History and Individualized Learning Projects) are specifically for advanced independence.

This book was designed to do more than simply provide social studies projects for students. Its primary purpose is to help *teach* children how to *become* independent learners. The difference is in the way the projects are taught: the idea is to gradually supply students with the skills they need for learning on their own as they study social studies topics. Teaching children to be independent learners is not easy, but it is important. As these projects are presented, try to keep in mind that nobody has the power to know what *facts* students will need twenty years from now, but there is little doubt that they will benefit for the rest of their lives from independent learning skills.

THE SKILLS CHART

Social Studies Projects is based upon skill development. The projects are arranged according to the amount of independence required, and a list of skills is provided for every project in the book. A comprehensive Skills Chart is included here to help define the skill requirements of each project. Many of them are basic, common sense skills that are already being taught in your classes.

The Skills Chart is divided into seven general skill areas: research, writing, planning, problem solving, self-discipline, self-evaluation, and presentation. Reading is not included on the chart because it is assumed that reading skills will be used with virtually every project.

The key tells if a skill is prerequisite (#), primary (X), secondary (O), or optional (*) for each project in the book. These designations are based upon the way the projects were originally taught; you may want to shift the skill emphasis of a project to fit the needs of your particular group of students. It is entirely up to you to decide how to present a project and what skills to emphasize. The Skills Chart is only a guide.

Examination of the chart quickly shows which skills are important to a project and which ones may be of secondary value. A project may be changed or rearranged to redirect its skill requirements. The projects in this book are designed to *teach* the use of skills. If a project's Teacher Preview lists twenty skills, but you want to emphasize only three or four of them, that is a perfectly legitimate use of the project.

Evaluating students on their mastery of skills often involves subjective judgments; each student should be evaluated according to his or her *improvement* rather than by comparison with others. Several projects supply evaluation forms to help with this process. In addition, the Teacher's Introduction to the Student Research Guide provides evaluations for notecards, posters, and oral presentations.

A blank Skills Chart is included at the end of the Student Research Guide in the Appendix. This chart can be helpful in several ways:

- Students can chart their own skill progression through a year. Give them a chart and tell them to record the title of a project on the first line. Have them mark the skills *you* have decided to emphasize with the project. This way, students will see *exactly* which skills are being taught and which ones they are expected to know how to use. As projects are continued through the year, the charts will indicate skill development.

- Use the chart to organize the skill emphasis of projects that did not come from this book. Quite often, projects have the potential to teach skills but they are not organized to do so. An entire course or even a curriculum can be organized according to the skill development on the chart.

- The Skills Chart can be used as a method of reporting to parents. By recording the projects and activities undertaken during a marking period in the left-hand column, a mark for each of the 49 skills can be given. For example, a number system can be used:

    1- excellent
    2- very good
    3- good
    4- fair
    5- poor

- A simpler method of reporting to parents is to give them a copy of the Skills Chart without marks and use it as the basis for a discussion about skill development.

Finally, most teachers have little or no experience teaching some of the skills listed on the chart. There is plenty of room for experimentation in the field of independent learning, and there are no established "correct" methods of teaching such things as problem solving, self-evaluation, and self-discipline. These are things that *can* be taught, but your own teaching style and philosophy will dictate how you choose to do it. Upon reflection, the skills listed on this chart should be recognizable as things that are worth teaching, even if you have not previously emphasized them.

SKILLS CHART: SOCIAL STUDIES

#	Prerequisite Skills — Students must have command of these skills.
X	Primary Skills — Students will learn to use these skills; they are necessary to the project.
O	Secondary Skills — These skills may play an important role in certain cases.
*	Optional Skills — These skills may be emphasized but are not required.

	RESEARCH									WRITING						PLANNING				
	PREPARING BIBLIOGRAPHIES	COLLECTING DATA	INTERVIEWING	WRITING LETTERS	LIBRARY SKILLS	LISTENING	MAKING NOTECARDS	OBSERVING	SUMMARIZING	GRAMMAR	HANDWRITING	NEATNESS	PARAGRAPHS	SENTENCES	SPELLING	GROUP PLANNING	ORGANIZING	OUTLINING	SETTING OBJECTIVES	SELECTING TOPICS
WHO'S IN THE NEWS	*	X			O	X	X	O	X	O	X	X	O	O	X		O			X
NEWSPAPER COLLAGES	*	X	*	*	O	X	*	X	*	O	O	X	O	O	O		X		*	X
CURRENT ARCHAEOLOGY	*	*	*		*	X	*	X	O	O	O	X	X	O	X	X	X			X
THE U.S.S.R.	*	X			O		*	O	X	O	X	X	X	X	X	*	X	O	O	X
GEOGRAPHY		X				X		X			X	X			O		X			
HISTORICAL STUDY	X	X	*	*	X	X	X	O	X	X	X	X	X	X	X	*	X	O	X	X
FAMOUS PEOPLE	X	X	*	*	X	X	X	O	X	X	X	X	X	X	X	*	X	*	O	X
EARLY AMERICAN HISTORY	X	X	*	*	X	X	X	O	X	X	X	X	X	X	X	X	X	O	X	X
INDIVIDUALIZED LEARNING PROJECTS	#	X	*	*	#	X	#	X	X	#	X	X	#	#	X	*	X	X	X	X
OPEN HOUSE	#	#	O	O	#	O	#	X	X	#	X	X	#	#	#	O	X	X	X	X

SKILLS CHART: SOCIAL STUDIES

PROBLEM SOLVING						SELF-DISCIPLINE										SELF-EVALUATION				PRESENTATION								
BASIC MATHEMATICS SKILLS	DIVERGENT-CONVERGENT-EVALUATIVE THINKING	FOLLOWING & CHANGING PLANS	IDENTIFYING PROBLEMS	MEETING DEADLINES	WORKING w/LIMITED RESOURCES	ACCEPTING RESPONSIBILITY	CONCENTRATION	CONTROLLING BEHAVIOR	FOLLOWING PROJECT OUTLINES	INDIVIDUALIZED STUDY HABITS	PERSISTENCE	SHARING SPACE	TAKING CARE OF MATERIALS	TIME MANAGEMENT	WORKING WITH OTHERS	PERSONAL MOTIVATION	SELF-AWARENESS	SENSE OF "QUALITY"	SETTING PERSONAL GOALS	CREATIVE EXPRESSION	CREATING STRATEGIES	DIORAMA & MODEL BUILDING	DRAWING/SKETCHING/GRAPHING	POSTER MAKING	PUBLIC SPEAKING	SELF-CONFIDENCE	TEACHING OTHERS	WRITING
				X	O	X	O	O	X	X	O			O		X	O	O	O	O	O		*	*	O	O	X	
	X	O		O	O	O	O	X	X	O	O	X	X	O		X	O	X	O	X	O		*	X	O	O	X	
	O	O		X	O	O	O	X	X	O	X	X	O	X	X	X	O	X	O	X	O	X	X			O	O	X
	O	O	O	X	O	X	X	X	X	O	X	X	O			X	O	X	O	O	O		*	X	X	X	X	X
X		O	O			X	X	X			X	X	X			X	O	X				X	*	*			*	
	X	O	O	X	O	X	X	X	X	X	X		O	X	*	X	X	X	X	O	X	*	*	*	X	X	X	X
	O	O	O	X	O	X	X	X	O	X	X	O	O	O	*	X	O	X	O	O	O	*	*	*	X	*		X
	X	X	X	X	X	X	X	X	X	X	X	X	X	X	X	X	X	X	X	X	X	*	X	X	*	X	X	X
	X	X	X	X	X	#	X	#	#	#	X	X	X	X	*	#	X	X	X	X	X	X	X	X	X	X	X	X
*	X	X	X	X	X	#	X	#	#	#	X	X	X	X	O	#	X	X	X	X	#	X	X	#	#	X	X	X

Contents

CONTENTS

"Readers' Guide to Periodical Literature"
"Choosing a Subject"
"Audio-Visual and Written Information Guides"
"Where to Go or Write for Information"
"Project Fact Sheet"
"Project Fact Sheet: Example"
"Poster Display Sheet"
"Things to Check Before Giving Your Presentation"
"Visual Aids for the Oral Presentation"
"Things to Remember When Presenting Your Project"
"Daily Log"
"Skills Chart" (blank)

WHO'S IN THE NEWS BULLETIN BOARD

Teacher Preview

Length of Project: 2 hours

Level of Independence: Basic

Goals:

1. To introduce students to current events.
2. To provide students with a homework project.
3. To produce a class bulletin board.

During This Project Students Will:

1. Choose a person from current events to study.
2. Follow an outline to produce one or two notecards of information.
3. Find a photograph or draw a picture of the person chosen.
4. Present their information to the class before placing notecards and pictures on the bulletin board.

Skills:

Collecting data	Selecting topics
Listening	Meeting deadlines
Making notecards	Accepting responsibility
Summarizing	Following project outlines
Handwriting	Individualized study habits
Neatness	Personal motivation
Spelling	Teaching others

Handout Provided:

- "Student Assignment Sheet"

PROJECT CALENDAR:

HOUR 1:_____	HOUR 2:_____	HOUR 3:_____
Introduction to the project; a due date is set for presentations. Discussion of people in the news.	Students "introduce" people from current events to the class.	
HANDOUT PROVIDED	STUDENTS TURN IN WORK	
HOUR 4:_____	**HOUR 5:**_____	**HOUR 6:**_____
HOUR 7:_____	**HOUR 8:**_____	**HOUR 9:**_____

Lesson Plans and Notes

HOUR 1: Give students their handouts and explain the parameters of the project. Set a due date and have students write this date on their handouts, then discuss a few examples of people in the news.

Notes:

- It's a good idea to exclude certain areas, such as sports and entertainment, from this project if you want to concentrate on current events. Consider the possibility of doing a second bulletin board on nothing *but* sports and entertainment personalities.

- The project is designed to let each student choose someone to study independently. This could lead to several students choosing the same person, however, so it is wise to provide an incentive to select a person that no one else is studying. Try this: Offer five "bonus" points to every student whose topic selection is unique. Post a list in the classroom that shows selections as they are made. This will prevent most problems with duplicates.

HOUR 2: Students bring their notecards and pictures to school on the due date. Each student presents his or her information to the class, and then places the notecards and picture on a bulletin board.

Note:

- Bulletin board space is needed for this hour. One way to display students' material is to place all of the pictures in the center of the bulletin board, like a collage, and surround them with notecards. Then run colored string from each card to the picture of the person it describes or give each card and corresponding picture a number so that students can tell who's who.

Name _____ Date _____

WHO'S IN THE NEWS BULLETIN BOARD
Student Assignment Sheet

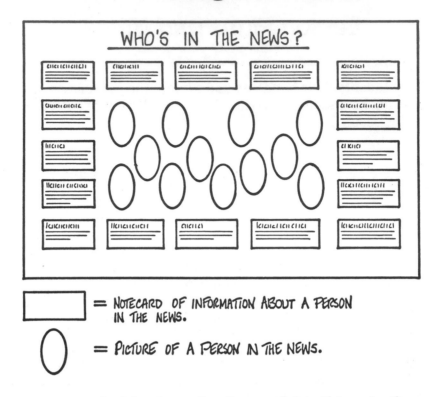

= NOTECARD OF INFORMATION ABOUT A PERSON IN THE NEWS.

= PICTURE OF A PERSON IN THE NEWS.

Every day you see news stories about people who are doing things in the world: politicians, world leaders, business people, religious leaders, police, criminals, scientists, doctors, and many, many others. By watching these people and listening to what they say, you can learn about current events. By choosing one person to study and "introducing" him or her to the class, you will help everyone understand a little more about current events.

This is a homework assignment: Follow the outline below and bring your completed work to class on the date set by your teacher.

DUE DATE: _____

I. Choose one person to study. This person must have been in the news at some time during the past twelve months.

II. Find a small picture (or draw one) of the person you have chosen to study.

III. In your best handwriting, record the following information on one or two notecards.

A. Your name
B. Name of the person you are studying
C. Title, position, or job that the person holds
D. Why the person is in the news
E. Date and name of the news source or sources
F. What country or state the person is from
G. Any other interesting facts you want to include

IV. On the due date that has been set by the teacher, you will "introduce" the person you studied to the class before placing your notecards and picture on the "Who's in the News" bulletin board.

NEWSPAPER COLLAGES

Teacher Preview

Length of Project: 10 hours

Level of Independence: Basic

Goals:

1. To introduce students to current events.
2. To make use of a ready source of information: newspapers.
3. To help students identify main ideas in news articles.
4. To emphasize divergent-convergent thinking.

During This Project Students Will:

1. Categorize news stories.
2. Create "divergent" collages of newspaper headlines.
3. Select news categories (one category per student)
4. Make "convergent" collages from articles they collect.
5. Identify main ideas or important facts in each of their articles.

Skills:

Collecting data	Following project outlines
Listening	Sharing space
Observing	Taking care of materials
Neatness	Personal motivation
Organizing	Sense of quality
Selecting topics	Creative expression
Divergent-convergent-evaluative thinking	Poster making
Controlling behavior	Teaching others

Handout Provided:

• "Student Assignment Sheet"

PROJECT CALENDAR:

HOUR 1:	HOUR 2:	HOUR 3:
Introduction to the project and discussion of recent newspaper articles.	Students receive a daily newspaper and clip headlines.	Students produce divergent collages.
PREPARATION REQUIRED HANDOUT PROVIDED	NEED SPECIAL MATERIALS	NEED SPECIAL MATERIALS STUDENTS TURN IN WORK
HOUR 4:	**HOUR 5:**	**HOUR 6:**
Students begin collecting material for the convergent collages.	Students continue collecting materials from newspapers.	Divergent collages are returned; students make convergent collages on the reverse side.
NEED SPECIAL MATERIALS	NEED SPECIAL MATERIALS	RETURN STUDENT WORK NEED SPECIAL MATERIALS
HOUR 7:	**HOUR 8:**	**HOUR 9:**
Students read articles and underline main facts.	Test writing begins.	Test writing is completed. Tests and convergent collages are handed in.
		STUDENTS TURN IN WORK

PROJECT CALENDAR:

HOUR 10: _____ Collages are returned. Students trade collages and tests to study each other's work. RETURN STUDENT WORK	**HOUR 11:** _____	**HOUR 12:** _____
HOUR 13: _____	**HOUR 14:** _____	**HOUR 15:** _____
HOUR 16: _____	**HOUR 17:** _____	**HOUR 18:** _____

Lesson Plans and Notes

HOUR 1: Give students the assignment sheet and explain the entire project. Spend the hour discussing various articles and headlines, and let the students decide how to categorize them.

Note:

- The project will go more smoothly if students first learn how to categorize headlines and articles. Display the front pages of several newspapers and refer to the headlines as you discuss local, state, national, and international news, and the various news categories that are listed on the student handout. If another hour is necessary to thoroughly explain categorization, it is time well spent.

HOUR 2: Give each student a daily newspaper. Students spend the hour clipping headlines for the divergent collage.

Notes:

- Each student will need a folder, scissors, a piece of *heavy* posterboard and a glue stick (or rubber cement) for Hours 2–6.
- If you contact your local newspaper several weeks in advance, it may be possible to obtain a free issue for each student on the day they begin the "divergent" collage. This way every student will be clipping the same material and you will know *exactly* what each person had to work with. Should this prove impractical, the project still works well with students using different issues of newspapers.

HOUR 3: Students arrange, paste, and label headlines on their collages. Collages are handed in at the end of the hour.

Note:

- Collect the "divergent" collages when they are completed and display them until they are returned to students at the beginning of the sixth hour. The project is designed to use *one* posterboard per student; the divergent collage is on one side and the convergent collage is then placed on the reverse side. It is advisable to use a *heavy* posterboard.

HOUR 4: Students choose (or are assigned) news categories for their convergent collages, and spend the hour searching through newspapers to find articles that relate to their categories. These articles are carefully dated and cut out.

Notes:

- For the *convergent* collage students must bring in newspapers from the past few weeks and months. Designate a three-day period for students to bring them in, supply a place to store them, and provide for their removal at the end of the project.

- For the convergent collage students will be sharing newspapers. It is important to emphasize that students should be careful when they cut articles from a newspaper: every article is potentially useful to someone in the class. Also, encourage students to share material that they find.

HOUR 5: Students continue searching for articles.

Note:

- You may want to add an hour to the project schedule and work with students on finding main ideas and important facts. This additional hour should be inserted between Hour 5 and Hour 6 of the project, before work begins on convergent collages.

HOUR 6: Divergent collages are returned. Students plan their convergent arrangements and paste them on the reverse side of the first collage. The rest of the hour (if time remains) is spent reading articles for main ideas and interesting facts.

HOUR 7: Students continue to read their articles and then underline main ideas and facts.

HOUR 8: Students begin creating tests for their collages.

Note:

- Some time should be spent teaching students how to write tests. The assignment handout explains how to make a matching test, but it is very important that students know how to identify *key* words or phrases for test items. If they choose inconsequential facts, the tests lose their meaning.

HOUR 9: Students complete their tests and hand them in along with collages.

Note:

- Students who finish early should be allowed to trade posters or to do touch-up work on their own collages before handing them in.

HOUR 10: Return the students' convergent collages. Have students trade collages and answer test questions.

Name _____ Date _____

NEWSPAPER COLLAGES
Student Assignment Sheet

Newspapers are an important source of news, information and opinion. Television has reduced the appeal of newspapers because it transmits information so quickly from anywhere in the world, but newspapers are still the best source of *in-depth* news. Students of social studies should be familiar with newspapers because they offer a close daily look at the present world.

This project is an exercise in divergent-convergent thinking that is designed to help you learn about current events. You will produce two newspaper collages. The first will be a "divergent" collage which shows headlines about *many different topics*. The second will be a "convergent" collage which shows as much information as possible about *one topic*.

Here is your assignment:

I.   DIVERGENT COLLAGE
A. For the divergent collage you will be given one newspaper to work with. Cut out as many headlines as you can find, and decide whether each describes a local, state, national, or international story. Then further categorize these headlines from the list below. It may be necessary to scan an article before deciding upon its category. When you paste a headline on the collage label it as a *local, state, national,* or *international* story, *and* record its news category. Some headlines may fit into more than one category. If so, use your best judgment.

1. Politics
2. Economics
3. Environment
4. Crime
5. Health/Medicine
6. Agriculture/Gardening
7. History/Archaeology
8. Religion
9. Education
10. Science
11. Military conflicts/Arms race
12. Terrorism
13. Government
14. Food/Nutrition
15. Industry/Business
16. Psychology
17. Human interest/Lifestyles
18. Human/Civil rights
19. Culture/Fine arts
20. Ethnic groups
21. Law
22. Weather
23. Travel
24. Fashion
25. Entertainment
26. Transportation
27. Accidents/Human tragedies
28. Technology
29. Sports/Leisure
30. Other _____

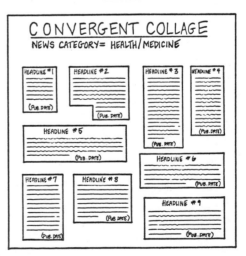

B. Put some thought into how you will arrange the collage before you begin pasting. Be sure all of the headlines are neatly trimmed.

C. Under each headline, on the posterboard, neatly print the category that best describes it. For example, this headline, "FOREST FIRE DESTROYS TOWN IN CHINA," would be labeled as an "International" news headline in the "Human tragedy" category.

D. Put your name on the *front* of the collage. The name and date of the newspaper you used should also be included.

II. CONVERGENT COLLAGE

A. For the convergent collage you will have access to many newspapers. Choose one of the news categories listed under item I of this handout and make the entire collage from articles and headlines about that topic area. Your teacher will tell you how to choose a category, so that many different topics are covered by the class.

B. Once you have selected a news category you will be given class time to search through newspapers to find articles for the collage. Be careful when you cut articles from the paper so that you don't destroy neighboring news stories which could be useful to your classmates. Include at least *five* articles in your collage.

C. Record the publication date of each article. Write this date on the article itself before you cut it out.

D. Follow these steps in planning and completing the collage:
1. Neatly trim all articles; be sure they are dated.
2. Write the name of your news category somewhere on the collage.
3. Before pasting, lay out your articles on the posterboard so that they look neat, and to ensure that space is used wisely.
4. When you are satisfied with the arrangement, begin pasting.
5. Add your own creative touches.
6. Put your name on the *front* of the collage.

III. LEARNING MORE ABOUT THE TOPIC

A. Read over the articles on your collage and underline *three* main ideas or interesting facts in each one.

B. Choose *one* of the things you have underlined from each article and write it on a piece of notebook paper. When you are finished, this paper will have one quote from every article on your collage. You will use these quotes to create a test.

C. Follow these steps to put together a test that asks at least *five* questions about your collage:
1. On your paper, underline one important word in each quote.
2. Recopy your notes, but leave a blank for each of the words you have underlined.
3. List the words that were underlined, in mixed order, at the bottom of the page.
4. The quotes with blanks become "matching" test questions, and the words become the possible answers. Add two or three extra words to your list so there are more answers than questions.
5. The news category and your name should be recorded at the top of the test paper.

D. Attach your test to the collage with a paper clip and hand it in.

CURRENT ARCHAEOLOGY

Teacher Preview

General Explanation:

For this project, students pretend to be archaeologists in the year 3000 A.D. They identify artifacts from the late twentieth century and build a museum with various theme rooms to display their findings. Findings come primarily from catalogs and newspapers.

Length of Project: 10 hours

Level of Independence: Basic

Goals:

1. To introduce students to the study of archaeology.

2. To encourage students to think about the importance of "ordinary" things in their lives.

3. To place emphasis upon imagination and creativity.

During This Project Students Will:

1. Discuss archaeology, artifacts, and how "ordinary" things tell us a lot about how people live.

2. Follow an outline to produce poster displays about artifacts from the late twentieth century.

3. Search through catalogs and newspapers to identify and collect modern "artifacts."

4. Produce signs to go with their artifact displays.

Skills:

Listening	Individualized study habits
Observing	Sharing space
Neatness	Taking care of materials
Paragraphs	Time management
Spelling	Working with others
Group planning	Personal motivation
Organizing	Sense of quality
Selecting topics	Creative expression

Meeting deadlines

Controlling behavior

Following project outlines

Drawing and sketching

Poster making

Writing .

Handout Provided:

- "Student Assignment Sheet"

PROJECT CALENDAR:

HOUR 1: _____ Introduction to the study of archaeology and discussion of what can be learned by studying artifacts. PREPARATION REQUIRED	**HOUR 2:** _____ Introduction to the project. Students are assigned to "rooms" in their class "museum." HANDOUT PROVIDED NEED SPECIAL MATERIALS	**HOUR 3:** _____ Students work in groups to cut pictures of "artifacts" from catalogs and newspapers. NEED SPECIAL MATERIALS
HOUR 4: _____ Group members each choose three artifacts to prepare for the museum room. 	**HOUR 5:** _____ Students complete their written material for the three artifacts each has chosen. STUDENTS TURN IN WORK	**HOUR 6:** _____ Students work on rough drafts of drawings for the museum display. STUDENTS TURN IN WORK
HOUR 7: _____ Written material and the rough drafts of drawings are returned. Students begin work on final posters. Work that must be rewritten or redrawn is done this hour. RETURN STUDENT WORK NEED SPECIAL MATERIALS	**HOUR 8:** _____ Students work on posters. NEED SPECIAL MATERIALS	**HOUR 9:** _____ Posters are completed by the end of the hour. NEED SPECIAL MATERIALS

PROJECT CALENDAR:

HOUR 10: _____ Students meet in their groups to arrange their display and make a sign for the finished exhibit. STUDENTS TURN IN WORK NEED SPECIAL MATERIALS	**HOUR 11:** _____	**HOUR 12:** _____
HOUR 13: _____	**HOUR 14:** _____	**HOUR 15:** _____
HOUR 16: _____	**HOUR 17:** _____	**HOUR 18:** _____

Lesson Plans and Notes

HOUR 1: Introduce students to the study of archaeology; include a presentation and discussion of a number of artifacts (or pictures of artifacts). Center the discussion on what we can learn from things used by people long ago. Ask the question: "What will people 1,000 years from now be able to tell about us from the things we use everyday?" Display, for discussion, such common items as a record album, a basketball, a piece of clothing, a tape recorder, an electronic toy, a "slinky," and so forth.

Note:

- Bring in three or four actual artifacts (you can get them on loan from a museum) or pictures of artifacts or antiques to help with your discussion. Discuss what these things tell us about the people who used them, or see if students can guess what they were used for.

HOUR 2: Give students the assignment sheet and explain the project point-by-point. Conduct a drawing to determine which museum "room" each student will make a display for. Spend the rest of the hour in small groups (each group represents a "room" in the museum) discussing exhibits and looking through catalogs.

Notes:

- Decide upon a way to get a number of catalogs for this project: department store catalogs work well. Ask students to bring them in and ask store managers about getting outdated catalogs. The more you have on hand the better. Ideally, you should have one for each student.

- The easiest way to conduct the drawing for museum rooms is to write areas of emphasis on slips of paper so that there is one slip for each student in your class. Put the slips in a hat and let each student draw one.

- There is a natural overlap in what might be included in each area of emphasis. One museum room may end up containing something that another room also contains. If this occurs it should not be viewed as a problem, but rather as an opportunity to discuss the interrelatedness of things.

HOUR 3: Students cut items from catalogs to use on their posters.

HOUR 4: Each group member chooses at least three artifacts from his or her group's collection. Students then work at their desks writing out the requirements for each artifact, as outlined in the handout.

HOUR 5: Students complete their written material for at least three artifacts by the end of the hour. This material must be handed in. Students who complete their written material before the end of the hour begin work on rough drafts of their three drawings.

Note:

- At the end of this hour students hand in rough drafts of written material. At the end of Hour 6 students hand in rough drafts of drawings. These things must be checked and handed back to students at the beginning of Hour 7.

HOUR 6: Students work on rough drafts of their drawings (although these are "rough" drafts, they should still be the students' best work). The drawings are handed in at the end of the hour.

HOUR 7: Written material and preliminary drawings are returned to students. Those who have adequately fulfilled the project requirements are given posterboards and begin laying out their displays. Those who have *not* done adequate work are required to spend the hour rewriting or redrawing.

HOUR 8: All students work on their posters.

HOUR 9: Students continue to work on their posters, which must be completed by the end of the hour.

HOUR 10: Students meet in their "museum room" groups to plan and make a sign for their exhibit before posters are put up for display. All posters and signs must be completed and on display by the end of this hour.

Name _____ Date _____

CURRENT ARCHAEOLOGY
Student Assignment Sheet

ARTIFACT FROM THE LATE 20TH CENTURY

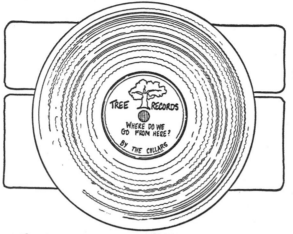

THIS DISC WAS CALLED A "RECORD ALBUM". IT CONTAINED MUSIC BUT NO VIDEO AND REQUIRED A MECHANICAL "NEEDLE" TO PICK UP THE SOUND FROM GROOVES.

Archaeology is the study of ancient history and the remains of former societies and cultures. For this project you will pretend to be an archaeologist in the year 3000 A.D. You have made a major discovery of artifacts that were buried in the last part of the twentieth century and you are now on assignment from the government to set up a museum display of the things you found.

The artifacts you have discovered are all items that can be found in a department store catalog. You will be given a catalog to work from, and your job is to search through it and cut out items to include in the museum display. Carefully follow the assignment outline below to satisfactorily complete this project:

I. The museum will be divided into several rooms, each with its own area of emphasis. A drawing will be conducted to determine which room your display will go into. Here is a list of the museum rooms:
   A. Electronics
   B. Tools
   C. Recreation/Entertainment
   D. Fashions
   E. Cooking and eating
   F. Home appliances and furniture
   G. Luxury items/Fads/Gadgets
   H. Other _____

II. Each museum room will be developed by three to five students. Each student will create a poster that shows several artifacts and explains how they were used. Your poster will relate to your museum room's area of emphasis.

III. Students who have drawn the same room assignment will get together to search for "artifacts" for their exhibit. In other words, they will look through catalogs and cut out pictures that may be used on their posters. After pictures are collected, you will be responsible for producing your own poster display, which becomes *part* of the total room exhibit.

IV. Follow these steps to complete a poster display:

A. Write your assigned museum room in this space: _____

_____

B. Write the names of the other students who have the same room assignment:

1. _____

2. _____

3. _____

4. _____

C. Meet with these students to collect pictures of "artifacts" and to discuss the exhibit.

D. Choose at least three of the group's collection of artifacts to include on your poster.

E. The poster should include the following information about *each* artifact:

1. The name of the artifact.
2. A picture of it from a catalog.
3. At least one drawing of how it was probably used. This drawing will be made by *you*.
4. A written description of how the artifact was used, to be placed beneath the drawing on the poster.
5. Approximate cost of the artifact: how much it cost when it was new.
6. A brief history of how and where the artifact was discovered. This should be written as a brief imaginary story.

V. When everyone's poster is completed, you and the other members of your group will make an exhibit "room" by combining your posters into a display in the classroom.

VI. Each group is responsible for designing and making a title sign to put above the exhibit produced by its members. For example: "Electronics from the Late 20th Century" or "The Cooking and Eating Room" or "Recreation and Entertainment from 1,000 Years Ago."

VII. Your grade for this project is based upon:

A. Following the project outline
B. Neatness
C. Completing the project on time
D. Working in a group and getting along with others
D. Taking care of materials
F. Effort

VIII. An example "artifact" report is provided here for your reference.
Sample artifact:

Name: Primitive Computer (circa 1990)

Drawing that shows its probable use:

Description of use:

It appears that there were many types of early computers. People apparently sat in front of them and pushed buttons or "keys" to talk to the computers. These crude machines were not intelligent and had to be continuously told what to do.

Approximate cost when new:

Like present-day matter transformers, early computers came in various price ranges. The one pictured above cost $850, but we have discovered remnant price lists that indicate a range of $200 to $5,000.

Brief history of how and where the artifact was discovered:

This primitive computer was accidentally stumbled upon by archaeologist Nextus Gilbert as he dug for the remains of a gigantic late twentieth century shopping mall on the outskirts of the ancient industrial city of Detroit.

THE U.S.S.R.:
STUDY OF A SUPERPOWER

Teacher Preview

Length of Project: 10 hours
Level of Independence: Basic
Goals:

1. To introduce students to the Soviet Union.
2. To place emphasis upon summarizing.
3. To help students learn how to understand the news they read each day.
4. To provide an opportunity to present and discuss current topics.

During This Project Students Will:

1. Use newspapers and magazines for research.
2. Select articles about the Soviet Union to study.
3. Identify main ideas in articles they have selected.
4. Summarize the main ideas from an article.
5. Present their summaries to the class.

Skills:

Collecting data	Selecting topics	Personal motivation
Summarizing	Working with limited resources	Sense of quality
Handwriting	Concentration	Poster making
Neatness	Controlling behavior	Public speaking
Paragraphs	Following project outlines	Self-confidence
Spelling	Individualized study habits	Teaching others
Sentences	Sharing space	Writing
Organizing	Taking care of materials	

Handout Provided:

• "Student Assignment Sheet"

PROJECT CALENDAR:

HOUR 1: _____	**HOUR 2:** _____	**HOUR 3:** _____
Introduction to the project. A date is set for students to bring in the newspapers and magazines needed for Hour 2.	Students conduct research in newspapers and magazines.	Research is continued.
HANDOUT PROVIDED	NEED SPECIAL MATERIALS	NEED SPECIAL MATERIALS
HOUR 4: _____	**HOUR 5:** _____	**HOUR 6:** _____
Students scan and evaluate their articles.	Students choose two articles from their research to work with and spend the hour reading them and underlining main ideas.	Poster layouts are planned and articles are pasted in place.
		NEED SPECIAL MATERIALS STUDENTS TURN IN WORK
HOUR 7: _____	**HOUR 8:** _____	**HOUR 9:** _____
Posters are returned and students summarize one of their two articles in writing.	Summaries are rewritten and pasted on posters.	Students present their summaries.
RETURN STUDENT WORK	NEED SPECIAL MATERIALS	STUDENTS TURN IN WORK

PROJECT CALENDAR:

HOUR 10: _____ Discussion of the information presented last hour, and about the U.S.S.R. in general. RETURN STUDENT WORK	**HOUR 11:** _____	**HOUR 12:** _____
HOUR 13: _____	**HOUR 14:** _____	**HOUR 15:** _____
HOUR 16: _____	**HOUR 17:** _____	**HOUR 18:** _____

Lesson Plans and Notes

HOUR 1: Give students the assignment sheet and explain the entire project. Set a date for students to bring newspapers and magazines to school and have them write this date on their handouts, under point I.

Notes:

- This project is dependent upon the materials that are supplied by students. Set a due date for these newspapers and magazines to be brought to school, but adjust your schedule so there is an extra day or two available for those who forget to bring materials in.
- Discuss with students what kinds of materials are necessary for this project: news magazines, newspapers, special journals, and the like.
- Discuss what a *main idea* is and what a *summary* is, and give examples. This is the crux of the project, and it is very important that students have a firm understanding of how to identify and summarize main ideas. You may want to cover these skills more thoroughly by presenting them to students before beginning the project.

HOUR 2: All resource material is in the classroom at the beginning of this hour. Each student is given a folder in which to store articles and the hour is spent finding and clipping articles that relate to the U.S.S.R. Scissors must be available.

Notes:

- You may want to provide a list of topics about which students will find articles during their search. This will help them better understand what they are looking for. For example:

  a. Nuclear policy and military issues
  b. Relations with the United States
  c. Human rights
  d. Food production/imports
  e. Space research/travel
  f. Military aid to other countries
  g. Current Soviet leader
  h. Presence in other countries
  i. Life in the Soviet Union
  j. Who's who in the Soviet Union

- Encourage students to cut articles out carefully, and then trim the edges neatly before putting them in folders. Scissors must be provided during Hours 2 and 3.

- Some students will bury themselves in the sports, comics, and fashion sections of the newspapers if you let them. Be prepared to deal with this when it happens, and set clear rules about it before beginning the project.

HOUR 3: Students continue to search for and cut out articles about the Soviet Union.

HOUR 4: Students scan and evaluate their articles in preparation for Hour 5. At the beginning of the next hour each student will choose two articles from his or her folder to work with.

HOUR 5: Each student chooses two articles and spends the hour reading them and underlining the main ideas. This assignment can be finished as homework.

Note:

- Establish a "class file" where students can store articles they choose not to use for their posters. This can be used by students who cannot find articles of their own. It can also be dated and used in succeeding years by future classes.

HOUR 6: Each student is given a small posterboard. Students plan their poster layouts and then paste articles (one per side) onto the posterboards. These are turned in at the end of the hour to be checked before students write summaries during Hour 7.

Notes:

- Rubber cement or glue sticks work best for "pasting" articles onto posterboard.
- The posterboard used for this project should be 14 x 22 inches (half of a regular posterboard). It is important to have all students working on the same size poster. This will make storage easier and ensure that nothing is lost. This is also why students are required to mount their articles before handing them in. (There should be a place in your classroom where posters this size can be stored.)
- The assignment calls for each student to choose two articles, underline the main ideas and then paste both articles on a posterboard, one to a side. These are handed in. Check to see that both articles are adequately underlined and suitable for summarizing. Students are required to summarize only one of their articles, but you may prefer to have them do one for practice and the other as a final project. Another option is to require those students who do a poor job on their first summary to do a second article summary.

HOUR 7: Posters are returned and each student spends the hour preparing a rough draft summary in his or her own words of one of the two articles. This assignment consists of two parts:

1. Students write single sentence summaries of at least five main ideas from their articles.

2. Students combine and rewrite their single sentence summaries into complete paragraphs.

These summaries will be rewritten in final draft form during the next hour.

Note:

- You may want to collect these rough drafts of the summaries and check them before the beginning of Hour 8. The assignment sheet tells students to write final drafts on their own, without handing rough drafts in.

HOUR 8: Students rewrite summaries in their best handwriting and paste them on posterboards. Students may want to take their posters home to practice for Hour 9, when summaries will be presented to the class.

HOUR 9: Students present their summaries to the class. Posters are turned in at the end of the hour.

HOUR 10: Return the students' posters and conduct a general discussion of the information brought in during Hour 9. Students may have questions or comments, and you will undoubtedly have points to make about the Soviet Union and the current world situation.

General Notes About This Project:

- A suggestion for expanding the scope of the project: include a vocabulary requirement. Students can be required to list all of the words in the articles that they do not know, and a composite class vocabulary list can be developed.

- Another suggestion: require a bibliography from each student for the two articles he or she has mounted on posterboard: name of the publication, author, date, page. (This means a bibliography of all articles clipped, since this information must be recorded before articles are cut out.)

- You may also want to include more research about the history and physical location of the Soviet Union. If so, place emphasis on geography, famous people, and historical events. You can show movies and filmstrips, require mini-research papers on specific topics taken from encyclopedias, or conduct map studies. There are many ways to expand this project, and it is recommended that you develop a format appropriate for your needs and your students' abilities.

THE U.S.S.R.: STUDY OF A SUPERPOWER
Student Assignment Sheet

The Soviet Union is in the news a lot these days. Because it is one of the largest, most powerful countries on earth, we must study it to understand world events. The initials "U.S.S.R." stand for "Union of Soviet Socialist Republics," which is usually shortened to "Soviet Union." Many people refer to it as "Russia," but in reality, Russia is only one of 15 republics that make up this communist country.

This project was designed to help you begin to learn about the Soviet Union and current events. You will be searching through newspapers and magazines to find articles that describe specific events or topics about the U.S.S.R. You won't be able to understand everything you find written in these articles because they may be too technical or require a knowledge of history. Some things, however, you *will* understand. The goal of the project is to introduce you to the U.S.S.R. and to show how this superpower influences world events.

Here is the project outline:

I. You and your classmates will be bringing newspapers and magazines to school. These will become your sources of information. Bring newspapers and magazines to school on this date: _____.

II. You will be given two hours of class time to search through the news materials for articles about the Soviet Union.

III. You will cut out articles that relate to the Soviet Union, and store them in a folder. Be sure to *scan* articles for references to the U.S.S.R.: headlines may not tell you specifically that an article contains information about the Soviet Union.

IV. From your folder of articles you will choose *two* that especially interest you. Be selective and choose articles that you can work with. These two articles will be kept in your folder and the rest of your articles will be placed in a class file.

V. Find and underline at least five main ideas in each article. If an article does not have five main ideas it is not suitable for this project. Be very careful as you read and mark the articles: don't mark anything until you have read the article thoroughly, then go back and underline *lightly* in pencil. Reread each article, and if you are convinced that you have properly underlined the main ideas, underline them again with ink or a fine line marker.

VI. You will be given a piece of posterboard on which to paste the articles. One article will go on one side of the poster and the other article will go on the opposite side. Position them so that there is also room for two half-sheets of lined paper on each side of the poster. Paste your articles on the posterboard, and turn it in to the teacher. The half-sheets of lined paper, which show how you summarized the article, will be written and mounted later. Your teacher will check to see that you have done a good job of locating the main ideas in the articles. You will complete the remainder of the project when the poster is returned.

VII. Your teacher may tell you which article to work with. If not, choose *one* and rewrite the main ideas into single sentence summaries. These idea summaries must be in your own words. Number each sentence and write at least five. When you are satisfied with your main idea summaries, rewrite them in your best handwriting on a half sheet of lined paper.

VIII. Write a one-paragraph rough draft which contains all of the main idea summaries. This is a summary of the entire article. Rewrite this paragraph in your best handwriting on a half-sheet of lined paper. Paste this final draft paragraph, along with the single sentence summaries, onto the posterboard. The poster should look something like this:

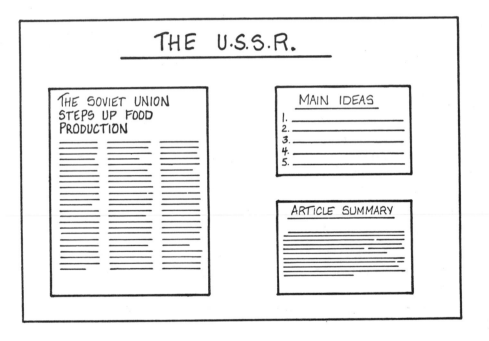

IX. Present your article summary orally to the class.
X. Turn your poster in to the teacher to be graded.
XI. You may continue this project by repeating numbers VII, VIII, IX, and X for the second article on the other side of the poster.

GEOGRAPHY

Teacher Preview

Project Topics:

World Study: The Continents (Hours 1–8)
Coordinate Systems (Hours 9–14)
Coordinate Mapping (Hours 15–17)
Review and Final Test (Hours 18–20)

General Explanation:

This project is divided into the three areas listed, plus a review and final test. Each of these areas can be taught as a separate project, but they are presented here as 20 continuous hours of instruction and activities, which is essentially a four-week geography unit. The lesson plans and notes describe how to teach each hour's course material. The handouts and tests provided follow the lesson plans, in the order they are to be given to students. Answers to homework assignments, class activities, and tests are located at the end of the instructional material.

Length of Project: 20 hours
Level of Independence: Basic
Goals:

1. To give students an orientation to the physical world in which they live.
2. To teach students a set of common geography terms.
3. To show students what coordinate systems are.
4. To show students how coordinate systems are used to map the world.

During This Project Students Will:

1. Identify and study the continents.
2. Locate specific places, areas, or physical features on unlabeled desk maps.
3. Define at least 21 geography terms.
4. Locate points using paired numbers in an X-Y coordinate system.
5. Study longitude and latitude, and see how they are used to form a coordinate system for mapping.
6. Create simple maps by following instructions from the teacher.

Skills:

Collecting data	Concentration
Listening	Controlling behavior
Observing	Individualized study habits
Handwriting	Persistence
Neatness	Taking care of materials
Organizing	Personal motivation
Basic mathematics skills	Sense of quality
Accepting responsibility	Drawing/Sketching/Graphing

Handouts Provided:

- "Geography Vocabulary"
- "4-Across Take-Home Games 1–4: Number Pairs" (answers provided)
- "4-Across Take-Home Games 5–8: Direction and Distance" (answers provided)
- "Coordinate Mapping Activity Sheet" (answers provided)
- "Geography Final Test" (answers provided for Parts I, II, and III)

PROJECT CALENDAR:

HOUR 1: _____	**HOUR 2:** _____	**HOUR 3:** _____
Introduction to the project; students receive the "Geography Vocabulary" handout. Work begins on unlabeled desk maps of Europe.	Students work on maps of Africa.	Students work on maps of Asia.
PREPARATION REQUIRED NEED SPECIAL MATERIALS HANDOUT PROVIDED STUDENTS TURN IN WORK	PREPARATION REQUIRED NEED SPECIAL MATERIALS RETURN STUDENT WORK STUDENTS TURN IN WORK	RETURN STUDENT WORK PREPARATION REQUIRED NEED SPECIAL MATERIALS STUDENTS TURN IN WORK
HOUR 4: _____	**HOUR 5:** _____	**HOUR 6:** _____
Students work on maps of the Middle East.	Students work on maps of North America.	Students work on maps of South America.
RETURN STUDENT WORK PREPARATION REQUIRED NEED SPECIAL MATERIALS STUDENTS TURN IN WORK	RETURN STUDENT WORK PREPARATION REQUIRED NEED SPECIAL MATERIALS STUDENTS TURN IN WORK	RETURN STUDENT WORK PREPARATION REQUIRED NEED SPECIAL MATERIALS STUDENTS TURN IN WORK
HOUR 7: _____	**HOUR 8:** _____	**HOUR 9:** _____
Students work on maps of Australia.	Students work on maps of the world.	Introduction to coordinate systems: students play the game 4-Across on the board or on an overhead transparency, using number pairs to locate points.
RETURN STUDENT WORK PREPARATION REQUIRED NEED SPECIAL MATERIALS STUDENTS TURN IN WORK	RETURN STUDENT WORK PREPARATION REQUIRED NEED SPECIAL MATERIALS STUDENTS TURN IN WORK	PREPARATION REQUIRED RETURN STUDENT WORK

PROJECT CALENDAR:

HOUR 10: _____	HOUR 11: _____	HOUR 12: _____
4-Across is played on the board using number pairs to locate points.	Students play 4-Across at their desks on graph paper, using number pairs to locate points. Optional homework assignment.	4-Across is played on the board, this time using *direction* and *distance* to locate points, rather than number pairs.
PREPARATION REQUIRED	NEED SPECIAL MATERIALS HANDOUT PROVIDED	PREPARATION REQUIRED
HOUR 13: _____	HOUR 14: _____	HOUR 15: _____
4-Across is played on the board, using direction and distance to locate points.	Students play 4-Across at their desks on graph paper, using direction and distance to locate points. Optional homework assignment.	Introduction to the use of a coordinate system to locate an *area* rather than a point: mapping.
PREPARATION REQUIRED	NEED SPECIAL MATERIALS HANDOUT PROVIDED	PREPARATION REQUIRED
HOUR 16: _____	HOUR 17: _____	HOUR 18: _____
Students locate places (areas) on a coordinate map that is drawn on the board or on an overhead transparency.	Students work on coordinate maps at their desks on graph paper.	Review for final test.
PREPARATION REQUIRED	PREPARATION REQUIRED NEED SPECIAL MATERIALS STUDENTS TURN IN WORK HANDOUT PROVIDED	RETURN STUDENT WORK

PROJECT CALENDAR:

HOUR 19: _____	HOUR 20: _____	HOUR 21: _____
Final Test	Return graded tests; discussion of the test.	
HANDOUT PROVIDED	RETURN STUDENT WORK	
HOUR 22: _____	HOUR 23: _____	HOUR 24: _____
HOUR 25: _____	HOUR 26: _____	HOUR 27: _____

Lesson Plans and Notes

World Study: The Continents (Hours 1–8)

HOUR 1: At the beginning of the hour give students the "Geography Vocabulary" handout. They are responsible for studying these terms for the final test, and being familiar enough with them to use them during class discussions.

These first eight hours of the course are basic practice in becoming familiar with world geography. Each hour give every student a map of one continent and a set of *sharp* colored pencils (fine-line markers or plain lead pencils will work). List 25 to 30 places from a specific area of the world on the chalkboard, and point them out, one at a time, on a large wall map. Have students locate these places on their desk maps, trace their outlines or borders, and carefully and neatly label them. A list of places is supplied with the "Geography Test," but it is partial and, for this activity, needs to be supplemented by you, depending upon what features or locations on each continent you want to emphasize. Europe is covered during this first hour. At the end of the hour, maps are turned in to be checked. At the beginning of the next hour these maps are returned to students.

Notes:

- Students will need desk maps for Hours 1–8 of instruction. These maps should be *unlabeled,* because you are going to ask students to carefully locate and mark 30 specific places on each one. Have one desk map of each continent (except Antarctica), plus a map of the Middle East, and the world, for each student in your class. You will need extra copies of these maps for the final test: one copy of the world map per student but only about five copies of each continent map. This will provide enough for a class of 35 students since each student is tested on just *one* of the continent maps, not on all of them. You will also need a large wall map of the world, or separate wall maps of the continents, to show students where places are located as they label their desk maps during Hours 1 through 8.

- Inform students that part of their final test will be two unlabeled desk maps and a list of 15 places that they will have to locate on each one. One of these maps will be a world map and the other will be one of the continent maps. Students do not know which continent map they will receive, so they must study all of their maps to do well on this part of the test.

- You may want to spend time in class going over vocabulary terms and pointing out examples on a wall map. Be sure to adjust the project schedule to allow time for discussing terms and definitions if you want to present them to students in class. New terms can be added to the list.

- An example of how a map study of Europe might be conducted is provided here for your reference. The teacher is being quoted:

WORLD STUDY: EUROPE (Example)

"This project is designed to help you learn about places in Europe. I have a list of 30 places, which I will write on the board one at a time. After I write the name of each place, I will point out on my wall map where that place is, and you will locate it on your desk map. After locating each place, neatly outline it, or color it in, *and* label it with its proper name. You may use arrows to help locate certain places precisely and to keep the map from becoming cluttered. At the end of the hour I will collect your map and grade it for accuracy, neatness, and spelling."

Places in Europe:

Adriatic Sea	Danube River	Poland
Aegean Sea	East Germany	Portugal
Alps Mountains	English Channel	Pyrenees Mountains
Atlantic Ocean	France	Rhine River
Baltic Sea	Greece	Rome
Bay of Biscay	Italy	Spain
Berlin	London	Strait of Gibraltar
Black Sea	Mediterranean Sea	U.S.S.R. (Soviet Union)
British Isles	Norway	Warsaw
(United Kingdom)	Paris	West Germany
Caspian Sea		

HOUR 2: Return the students' maps of Europe from Hour 1, then have them work on desk maps of Africa, locating 30 places that you specify. Your list should include 15 places from the final test and 15 additional places, chosen according to what you want to emphasize. The notes supplied for Hour 1 apply equally to this and to the next six hours. Continue collecting and returning work, using the pattern developed in Hours 1 and 2.

HOUR 3: Students work on desk maps of Asia.

HOUR 4: Students work on desk maps of the Middle East.

HOUR 5: Students work on desk maps of North America.

HOUR 6: Students work on desk maps of South America.

HOUR 7: Students work on desk maps of Australia.

HOUR 8: Students work on desk maps of the world.

General Notes on "World Study: The Continents":

• A list of 15 places for each continent is provided as part of the final test. Be sure to use these places as you create your list of 30. It is left to you to decide which 15 additional places students should learn about and locate on each map; this gives you control over the focus of their study. Try to include countries, cities, rivers, seas, gulfs, and territories that are currently in the news, or that have historic significance, so that students can see some purpose in learning about the geography of the world.

- The "Geography Test" that is provided includes a "match-up" quiz of all the terms and definitions on the student handout. It also has a section on the continents: each student is given a desk map of the world *and* a desk map of one of the continents. *Everyone* works on his or her world map to locate and mark the 15 places listed in part IV of the test. The second map for each student may be North America, South America, Europe, Africa, Asia, Australia, or the Middle East. Students do not know which of these maps they will get with their tests, so they must study all of them.

- Locating places on maps can be somewhat mundane, but its purpose is important: to introduce students to the world they live in. You can add to the project by allowing students to color their maps and neatly outline such natural features as mountain ranges, deserts, rivers, and lakes. Emphasize neatness throughout these first eight hours, and insist on good handwriting and spelling from students.

Coordinate Systems (Hours 9–14)

HOUR 9: Before class begins, draw a graph on the board (or on an overhead transparency) with spaces of about 10 centimeters and a vertical axis and a horizontal axis in different colors. (This forms an X-Y coordinate system, but you need not even introduce the two variables. "X" and "Y" are often confused with "X" and "O," which are used in the game. Students will learn to locate points using *number pairs*). Tell students that they are going to play a game on the board called "4-Across." Divide the class in half, and give instructions for the game, as follows:

1. One team is X's and the other is O's. X starts the game.
2. Explain that the object of the game is for one team to get four marks in a row: horizontally, vertically, or diagonally. There is one catch, however: students must figure out for themselves why the marks are being placed where they are by the teacher.
3. The first person in the first row on the "X's" side is told to call out a number pair; neither number can be larger than 10. (You must have at least ten lines on each side of both axes).
4. The teacher marks this point on the coordinate system with an "X," and writes the number pair on the board.
5. The first person in the first row on the "O's" side is told to call out a number pair; the teacher marks this point with an "O" and writes the number pair on the board.
6. The turn goes back and forth between "X" and "O" until one team wins with four marks in a row.
7. There can be no talking during the game.

　　　As students gradually figure out the system, competition intensifies. However, the game is usually played only in the upper right-hand quadrant, because this is where all the positive numbers are. If nobody has cracked the negative number barrier after the second or third game, add an eighth rule: no point will be marked on the game board unless it is located in one of the other quadrants. Tell them to *think* about it; they'll figure it out. Play as many games as can be squeezed into an hour. Here's how points are marked.

　　　A number pair is written like this: (6, 3). The first number (the "X" coordinate) tells how far to go *right* or *left* on the graph from the middle, the (0, 0) point. A positive number goes right and a negative number goes left. The second number (the "Y" coordinate) tells how far to go *up* or *down* on the graph from the middle, the (0, 0) point. A positive number goes up and a negative number goes down.

Examples:

(6, 3) right 6; up 3

(−6, 3) left 6; up 3

(6, −3) right 6; down 3

(−6, −3) left 6; down 3

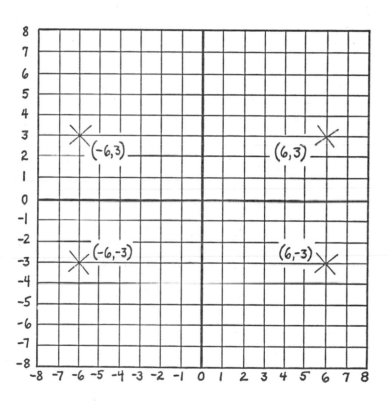

Notes:

- If you are not familiar with Cartesian coordinates (locating points on an X-Y axis), review the material in this section carefully before beginning to teach about coordinate systems.

- When working with coordinate systems, it is important to realize that number pairs locate points from the origin (0,0). This is where the horizontal and vertical axes cross.

HOUR 10: Students play 4-Across again. This time, however, the teams alternate, with each student going in turn to the board, writing out a number pair and marking the point correctly. Through its "captain" or "leader," the other team can challenge a mark that it feels is incorrectly placed. An incorrect mark is erased, and that team loses its turn. Silence is absolutely necessary. Before the hour begins, a graph must be drawn on the board. This preparation is also required for Hours 12, 13, 15, and 16.

HOUR 11: Students play 4-Across one-on-one at their desks on graph paper. The requirement of writing down number pairs before marks are made still holds, and moves can be challenged to a "judge" (either a student or teacher).

Notes:

- A supply of graph paper should be available for the 4-Across games that students play in class and for the final test.
- There are four games of 4-Across (games 1–4, using number pairs) provided for you to use as worksheets or homework assignments. Students record these moves as X's and O's on pieces of graph paper.

HOUR 12: The emphasis shifts from *positive and negative* numbers to *direction and distance* for the location of points on a coordinate system. Have students play 4-Across on the board again, but this time calling two coordinates [such as, "north 6 degrees" and "west 5 degrees" (N6°, W5°)] and with the teacher placing the marks on the board. The axes now represent the divisions between north, south, east, and west, and distance is measured in degrees of longitude and latitude. These two terms and what they represent should be explained during the first part of the hour. Points are located like this:

(N6°, W5°):	up 6; left 5
(N6°, E5°):	up 6; right 5
(S6°, W5°):	down 6; left 5
(S6°, E5°):	down 6; right 5

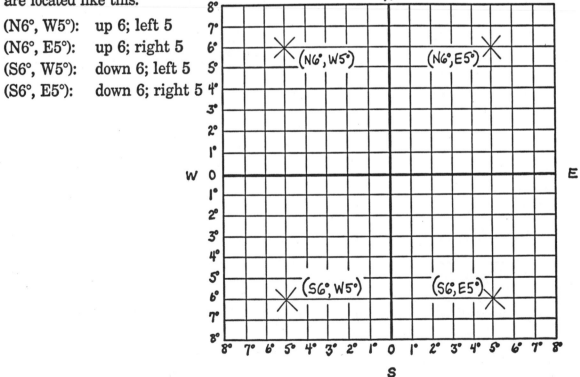

HOUR 13: Students play 4-Across on the board using direction and distance instead of positive and negative numbers. Each student in turn writes coordinates on the board and marks the point.

HOUR 14: Students play 4-Across at their desks. There are several take-home 4-Across games (games 5–8, which use direction and distance) included with this project that can be used to whatever extent is deemed necessary. Students record these moves (coordinates) as X's and O's on pieces of graph paper and then write down who won the game, X or O.

Coordinate Mapping (Hours 15–17)

HOUR 15: Introduce students to the idea that maps use latitude and longitude to tell where places are located on the surface of the earth. Each of these places is located in an *area*, a concept different from the idea of locating places at *points*, as has been done in classes up to now. Places on a map are located *between* lines of latitude and lines of longitude. For example, Lake Michigan is located *between* 86° and 88° west longitude, and *between* 41° and 46° north latitude. This concept is difficult for many students to understand, and it requires the first hour to demonstrate and illustrate on a chalkboard how a lake or a town can be located on a coordinate system, using direction and degrees of latitude and longitude.

Example:

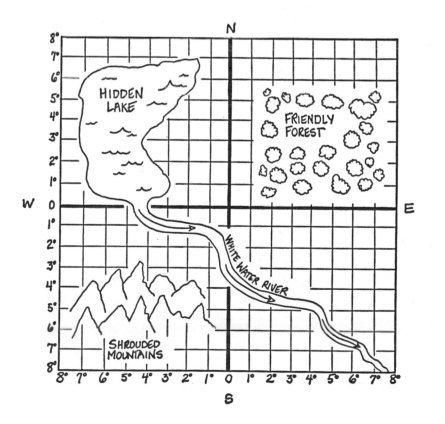

Notes:

- The purpose of this project is to show students how *areas* can be located on maps. You may be surprised at how difficult a process it will be for some students to grasp this. Be prepared to add an extra hour to the schedule if students need additional instruction.

- The concept of dividing degrees into minutes, and minutes into seconds, can also be very difficult for junior high and elementary students. The activities for this project involve making maps on graph paper that has been divided into quadrants by north-south and east-west axes. Each line represents one degree, and they are numbered in each direction from the center. In reality, one degree of longitude or latitude at the equator equals about 70 miles, so the scale on the maps being made in class is not accurate. If it were an accurate scale, the towns students draw would be on the order of 400–500 miles across, and roads would be 70 miles wide. The inconsistencies involved in working with a disproportionate scale are easier to explain, however, than how to work with minutes and seconds.

  Spend some time explaining that one degree on a real map represents a much longer distance than it does on the students' maps. If the term "minute" or "second" is to be used instead of degree, here are the real-scale equivalents:

  1 minute = 1.17 miles of latitude
  1 second = 0.02 miles of latitude

HOUR 16: Use a graph on the board or an overhead transparency, divided into quadrants, for this activity. It is not a game, and there are no teams. Randomly select students to go to the board and locate places on the coordinate map. Specify such locations as:

1. A forest between 6° and 8°N latitude and 4° and 7°W longitude.
2. A river between 8° and 10°W longitude.
3. A person standing at the intersection of 8°N latitude and 8°W longitude.
4. An airport between 5° and 7°S latitude and 3° and 4°E longitude.
5. Etc.

A lot of fun can be added to this activity by naming the places after students in the class. For example: "John Wilson, this map doesn't have the ancient and forbidding Wilson Forest on it, which is located between 6°N and 10°N, and 8°W and 14°W. Please go up and draw it on the map for us. Anne Schmidt, go up and show us where the famous River Schmidt is. I understand it's between 3°S and 5°S. Emily Johnson, where is Johnson Airport located?"...and so forth. For this activity you can make up coordinates for places as you watch the map develop on the board. There is no complete list included here.

Notes:

- Come to class prepared to give students coordinates for creating a map on the board. You may want to invent these coordinates spontaneously in class as you see the map develop on the board, or you may feel more comfortable designing your map on graph paper before class begins.
- You can also require students to draw this map at their desks on graph paper while individuals are at the board. This gives everyone something to do, and is a good way to prepare for the next hour's activity.

HOUR 17: At the beginning of the hour give everyone a sheet of graph paper which is ruled into four equal quadrants. It is placed on the desk with the holes on the left (long side of the paper right and left, short side top and bottom). From the front of the room, read students the coordinates for a variety of "places," which are provided on the "Coordinate Mapping Activity Sheet." Write these on the board as you give them. From these directions students are required to construct maps and label each place properly. Neatness is important! These maps are turned in at the end of the hour. Once again, some fun can be added by using students' names to identify the places on the map. The "Coordinate Mapping Activity Sheet" is included with the handouts for geography and can be given to students instead of reading the coordinates from the front of the room.

Review and Final Test (Hours 18–20)

HOUR 18: Set aside this hour to return and discuss maps from Hour 17, to answer questions, to go over areas that students had difficulty with, and to review information about continents, coordinate systems, and coordinate mapping. Tell students the kinds of things that will be on the final test.

HOUR 19: Students are given a final geography test, which is provided.

HOUR 20: Tests are returned and mistakes corrected.

GEOGRAPHY VOCABULARY

Bay: An inlet of the ocean or other large body of water, bordering on land and partly surrounded by land.

Canal: A man-made waterway for navigation, irrigation, or drainage.

Channel: A narrow strip of water.

Continent: Any one of the seven largest areas of land on the earth's surface.

Delta: Earth that is deposited by running water when a stream flows into a lake or ocean.

Gulf: An area of water lying within a curved coastline; usually larger than a bay and smaller than a sea.

Harbor: A sheltered body of water where ships anchor and are protected from storms.

Island: An area of land surrounded by water.

Isthmus: A narrow piece of land joining two larger bodies of land, or a peninsula with a mainland.

Latitude: Lines that run east and west and measure how far north or south of the equator you are.

Longitude: Lines that run north and south and measure how far east or west you are of the prime meridian.

Mountain range: A series of connecting mountains.

Oasis: A fertile spot within a desert region, watered by underground springs or irrigation.

Ocean: Any one or all of the five largest bodies of salt water on the earth's surface (Atlantic, Pacific, Indian, Arctic, and Antarctic).

Pass: An opening through hills or mountains used as a route for railroads, trails, and highways.

Peninsula: A piece of land nearly surrounded by water and attached to a larger area of land.

River mouth: The place where a river empties and ends its course.

River source: The place where a river begins.

Reef: A chain of rocks or coral, or ridge of sand, at or near the surface of water.

Sea: A large body of water partly or nearly surrounded by land.

Strait: A passageway of water connecting two large bodies of water.

Name _____ Date _____

4-ACROSS TAKE-HOME GAMES 1–4:
NUMBER PAIRS

Game 1

(X's)	(O's)
1. (−3,3)	2. (3,3)
3. (−2,2)	4. (−1,1)
5. (−2,3)	6. (−4,3)
7. (−1,3)	8. (0,3)
9. (−3,1)	10. (−4,0)
11. (0,4)	12. (4,4)

Game 2

(X's)	(O's)
1. (2,10)	2. (−6,−4)
3. (1,11)	4. (0,12)
5. (3,9)	6. (4,8)
7. (5,−2)	8. (−3,−1)
9. (5,−1)	10. (5,0)
11. (4,−1)	12. (3,0)
13. (6,−3)	14. (−4,−2)
15. (8,−4)	16. (−5,−3)

Game 3

(X's)	(O's)
1. (−5,−5)	2. (−5,−4)
3. (−4,−4)	4. (−3,−3)
5. (−4,−3)	6. (−4,−5)
7. (−4,−2)	8. (−4,−1)
9. (−5,−2)	10. (−3,−2)
11. (−3,−1)	12. (−5,0)
13. (−2,−3)	14. (−6,1)

Game 4

(X's)	(O's)
1. (0,0)	2. (5, −3)
3. (−1,1)	4. (1,−1)
5. (−2,2)	6. (−3,3)
7. (−3,2)	8. (−4,2)
9. (−2,4)	10. (−2,3)
11. (−4,3)	12. (−5,1)
13. (−6,0)	14. (3,−1)
15. (2,−1)	16. (4,−2)
17. (6,−4)	18. (0,2)
19. (2,0)	20. (2,−2)
21. (1,0)	22. (3,0)
23. (−1,0)	24. (5,−4)

OBJECT OF THE GAME:

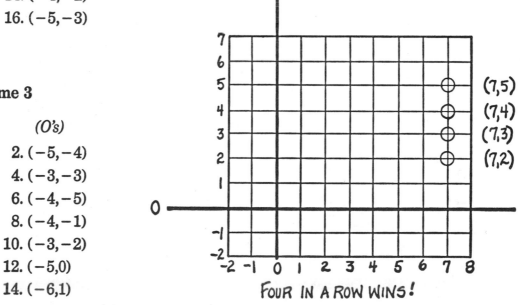

FOUR IN A ROW WINS!

45

4-ACROSS TAKE-HOME GAMES 5–8: DIRECTION AND DISTANCE

GAME 5

(X's)	(O's)
1. N3°; E3°	2. N3°; W3°
3. N2°; E2°	4. N1°; E1°
5. N3°; E2°	6. N3°; E4°
7. N3°; E1°	8. N3°
9. N1°; E3°	10. E4°
11. N4°	12. N4°; W4°

GAME 6

(X's)	(O's)
1. N10°; W2°	2. S4°; E6°
3. N11°; W1°	4. N12°
5. N9°; W3°	6. N8°; W4°
7. S2°; W5°	8. S1°; E3°
9. S1°; W5°	10. W5°
11. S1°; W4°	12. W3°
13. S3°; W6°	14. S2°; E4°
15. S4°; W8°	16. S3°; E5°

GAME 7

(X's)	(O's)
1. S5°; E5°	2. S4°; E5°
3. S4°; E4°	4. S3°; E3°
5. S3°; E4°	6. S5°; E4°
7. S2°; E4°	8. S1°; E4°
9. S2°; E5°	10. S2°; E3°
11. S1°; E3°	12. E5°
13. S3°; E2°	14. N1°; E6°

GAME 8

(X's)	(O's)
1. N0°; E0°	2. S3°; W5°
3. N1°; E1°	4. S1°; W1°
5. N2°; E2°	6. N3°; E3°
7. N2°; E3°	8. N2°; E4°
9. N4°; E2°	10. N3°; E2°
11. N3°; E4°	12. N1°; E5°
13. E6°	14. S1°; W3°
15. S1°; W2°	16. S2°; W4°
17. S4°; W6°	18. N2°
19. W2°	20. S2°; W2°
21. W1°	22. W3°
23. E1°	24. S4°; W5°

COORDINATE MAPPING ACTIVITY SHEET

Use these coordinates to construct a simple map on graph paper. Each item on this list locates an *area* which should be clearly outlined on your finished map. Label each area.

1. TOWN: Between 3° and 9° north, and 3° and 10° east

2. MAIN ROAD: Between 5° and 6° north

3. ROAD WORK CREW: Between 4° and 5° west, and between 5° and 6° north

4. CEMETARY: Between 9° and 10° north, and 10° and 11° east

5. RIVER: Between 1° and 6° south; the river flows east

6. OLD HERMIT'S CAVE: At the intersection of 14° west and 19° south

7. BRIDGE: Between 8° and 9° west, and between 1° and 6° south

8. FOREST: Between 14° and 20° south, and between 5° and 13° east

9. MOUNTAIN RANGE: Between 16° and 20° north, and between 8° and 13° west

10. LAKE: Between 12° and 19° north and between 6° and 12° east

11. ANCIENT TOWER: At the intersection of 11° south and 5° east

12. CORN FIELDS: Between 10° and 13° south and between 11° and 14° west

13. HAUNTED HOUSE: At the intersection of 9° north and 8° west

14. MILL POND: Between 6° and 8° south, and between 6° and 8° east

15. PERSON WALKING TO TOWN: At the intersection of 13° north and 3° east

Scoring for this project: intersections = 1 point each
area locations = 4 points each
Total: 51 points

GEOGRAPHY FINAL TEST

PART I: You have a piece of graph paper which will soon become a map of a make-believe country called Quasi-Land. Follow the instructions below carefully to locate the important landmarks and historical sites in Quasi-Land. Don't forget to do numbers 18–27 on the next page. Each one is worth one point.

1. Place your paper so the holes are on the left and draw two lines through the center of the map. One line is north-south; the other is east-west.
2. Creepy Swamp is located between 17° and 20°N and 5° and 10°E.
3. Fort Dill, Quasi-Land's main defense, is located between 11° and 16°W and 13° and 20°N.
4. There is a fresh water well at the intersection of 5°W and 3°N. Mark it with a small box and write "fresh H$_2$O."
5. The River Bos flows through Quasi-Land between 11° and 14°E. The water flows south. Draw the river and show which direction the water flows with an arrow.
6. The small town of Valentine is located on the west bank of the River Bos and is located between 9° and 11°E and 8° and 10°S. Find this area and mark it with a "V."
7. The highest point in Quasi-Land is on top of Mount Cloud at the intersection of 7°S and 15°W. Find this point, draw a triangle around it and label it "M.C."
8. The only bridge across the River Bos is located between 2° and 3°N. Draw the bridge on your map. Label it "Bridge."
9. The ancient ruins of a Middle Earth Fortress still remain in Quasi-Land. It is located between 5° and 7°N and 4° and 6°E. Show on your map where these ruins are by making a small drawing of a castle.
10. The place where the final battle for Quasi-Land's independence took place is at the intersection of 6°S and 9°E. Find this place, mark it with a capital "I," and draw a circle around it.
11. A town named Ontario is located between 3° and 6°W and 4° and 7°S. Find this area and mark it with an "O" inside a square.
12. The birthplace of Quasi-Land's first president is located at the intersection of 5°S and 4°E. Find this point and mark it with "P."
13. The most productive garden in all of Quasi-Land is located between 17° and 18°N and 2° and 3°W. Mark this area with a "G."
14. "The Trench" is a very important irrigation ditch in Quasi-Land. It is located between 17° and 19°S and 0° and 16°W. Draw it on your map and label it "The Trench."
15. The Quasi-Land Zoo is located between 11° and 13°W and 8° and 10°N. Find the zoo and mark it with a "Z."
16. Quasi-Land Farms is located in rich bottom lands, between 15° and 18°S and 7° and 11°E. Mark this area "Q-F."
17. Pickwick Pond can be found between 4° and 6°W and 11° and 13°S. Draw it and label it "PP."

18–27: Locate the homes of the ten wealthiest Quasi-Landians on your map of Quasi-Land by putting an "X" where the longitude and latitude lines intersect. (1 point each)

© 1987 by The Center for Applied Research in Education, Inc.

GEOGRAPHY FINAL TEST (continued)

	Longitude	Latitude			Longitude	Latitude
18.	3°E	2°N		23.	7°W	11°N
19.	2°E	4°S		24.	11°W	9°S
20.	7°E	13°S		25.	9°E	8°N
21.	4°W	2°S		26.	1°E	12°N
22.	13°W	5°N		27.	10°W	12°N

PART II: 4-Across. On a fresh piece of graph paper make the center lines for a "4-Across" game. Below are the moves which were made in a recent game. Play the game and put the marks "X" and "O" where they belong. Each mark is worth one point. Write on your paper which person won. "X" starts the game.

(X's)	(O's)
1. (−2,−1)	2. (−1,−1)
3. (−3,−1)	4. (−4,−1)
5. (−2, 0)	6. (−2, 1)
7. (−2, 2)	8. (−2,−3)
9. (−1,−2)	10. (0,−3)
11. (0,−2)	12. (1,−2)
13. (−3, 0)	14. (−4, 1)
15. (−3,−2)	16. (−3, 1)
17. (−2,−2)	18. (−3,−4)

PART III: In the left-hand column is a list of geography terms; in the right-hand column is a list of definitions. Place the letter of the correct definition beside each term. (1 point each)

1. ____ BAY

2. ____ CONTINENT

3. ____ GULF

4. ____ DELTA

5. ____ ISTHMUS

6. ____ ISLAND

7. ____ HARBOR

8. ____ CHANNEL

9. ____ CANAL

10. ____ RIVER SOURCE

11. ____ OASIS

12. ____ RIVER MOUTH

a. The place where a river empties and ends its course.

b. A sheltered body of water where ships anchor and are protected from storms.

c. An area of land surrounded by water.

d. The place where a river begins.

e. An inlet of the ocean or other large body of water, bordering on land, and partly surrounded by land.

f. A fertile spot within a desert region, watered by underground springs or irrigation.

g. A series of connecting mountains.

h. Earth that is deposited by running water when a stream flows into a lake or ocean.

i. An area of water lying within a curved coastline; usually larger than a bay and smaller than a sea.

j. A chain of rocks or coral, or ridge of sand, at or near the surface of water.

GEOGRAPHY FINAL TEST (continued)

13. ____ PASS

14. ____ SEA

15. ____ OCEAN

16. ____ MOUNTAIN RANGE

17. ____ PENINSULA

18. ____ REEF

19. ____ STRAIT

k. A piece of land nearly surrounded by water and attached to a larger area of land.

l. Any one, or all, of the five largest bodies of salt water on the earth's surface.

m. A large body of water partly or nearly surrounded by land.

n. A man-made waterway filled with water for navigation, irrigation, or drainage.

o. A narrow strip of water.

p. A passageway of water connecting two large bodies of water.

q. A narrow piece of land joining two larger bodies of land or a peninsula with a mainland.

r. An opening through hills or mountains used as a route for railroads, trails, and highways.

s. Any one of the seven largest areas of land on the earth's surface.

20. Write a good definition for *longitude*. (3 pts.)

21. Write a good definition for *latitude*. (3 pts.)

PART IV: Locate the following places on the world map which will be given to you. Each correct answer is worth one point. Mark them carefully.

1. Africa
2. South America
3. North America
4. Red Sea
5. Strait of Gibraltar
6. Gulf of Mexico
7. Pacific Ocean
8. Tropic of Cancer
9. Equator
10. Caspian Sea
11. Caribbean Sea
12. Bay of Bengal
13. Mexico
14. Greenland
15. Atlantic Ocean

GEOGRAPHY FINAL TEST (continued)

PART V: You will be given a map of *one* of the continents (or the Middle East). From the lists that follow, find the fifteen places for your continent and mark them carefully on the map. Each correct answer is worth one point.

PLACES TO LOCATE ON YOUR MAP

Asia
1. Philippine Islands
2. Korea
3. Vietnam
4. Bay of Bengal
5. India
6. Persian Gulf
7. Arabian Sea
8. Sea of Japan
9. Arctic Circle
10. Caspian Sea
11. Red Sea
12. Iran
13. Bering Sea
14. Pacific Ocean
15. Gulf of Tonkin

Middle East
1. Egypt
2. Red Sea
3. Persian Gulf
4. Iran
5. Gulf of Oman
6. Caspian Sea
7. Turkey
8. Afghanistan
9. Mediterranean Sea
10. Saudi Arabia
11. Jordan
12. Libya
13. Israel
14. Black Sea
15. Strait of Hormuz

North America
1. Alaska
2. Gulf of Mexico
3. Hudson Bay
4. Lake Michigan
5. Atlantic Ocean
6. Mississippi River
7. Cuba
8. Greenland
9. Pacific Ocean
10. Mexico
11. Baja California
12. Tropic of Cancer
13. Bering Strait
14. Canada
15. Gulf of Alaska

Australia
1. Great Barrier Reef
2. Great Australian Bight
3. Tasmania
4. Tasman Sea
5. New Guinea
6. Indian Ocean
7. Pacific Ocean
8. Tropic of Capricorn
9. Timor Sea
10. Queensland
11. New South Wales
12. Victoria
13. Bass Strait
14. Spencer Gulf
15. Gulf of Carpentaria

Europe
1. Caspian Sea
2. Black Sea
3. Aegean Sea
4. Mediterranean Sea
5. U.S.S.R.
6. Italy
7. Strait of Gibraltar
8. Spain
9. Adriatic Sea
10. France
11. Atlantic Ocean
12. Norway
13. Baltic Sea
14. Portugal
15. Bay of Biscay

Africa
1. Strait of Gibraltar
2. Mediterranean Sea
3. Sinai Peninsula
4. Egypt
5. Red Sea
6. Nile River
7. Libya
8. Tropic of Cancer
9. Madagascar
10. South Africa
11. Ethiopia
12. Somalia
13. Cape of Good Hope
14. Indian Ocean
15. Gulf of Guinea

South America
1. Caribbean Sea
2. Panama
3. Amazon River
4. Atlantic Ocean
5. Pacific Ocean
6. Indian Ocean
7. Equator
8. Chile
9. Rio de la Plata
10. Tropic of Capricorn
11. Falkland Islands
12. Strait of Magellan
13. Brazil
14. Argentina
15. Colombia

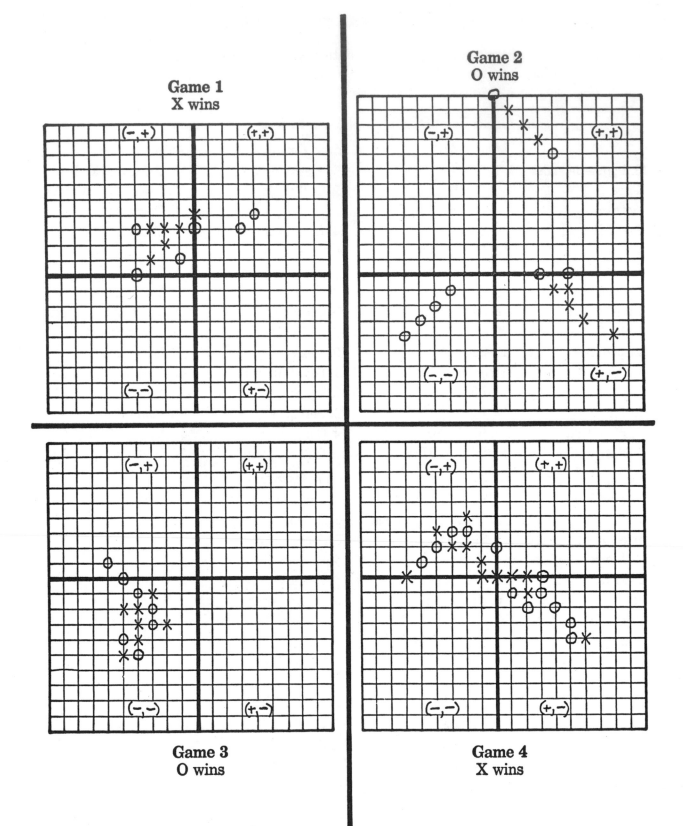

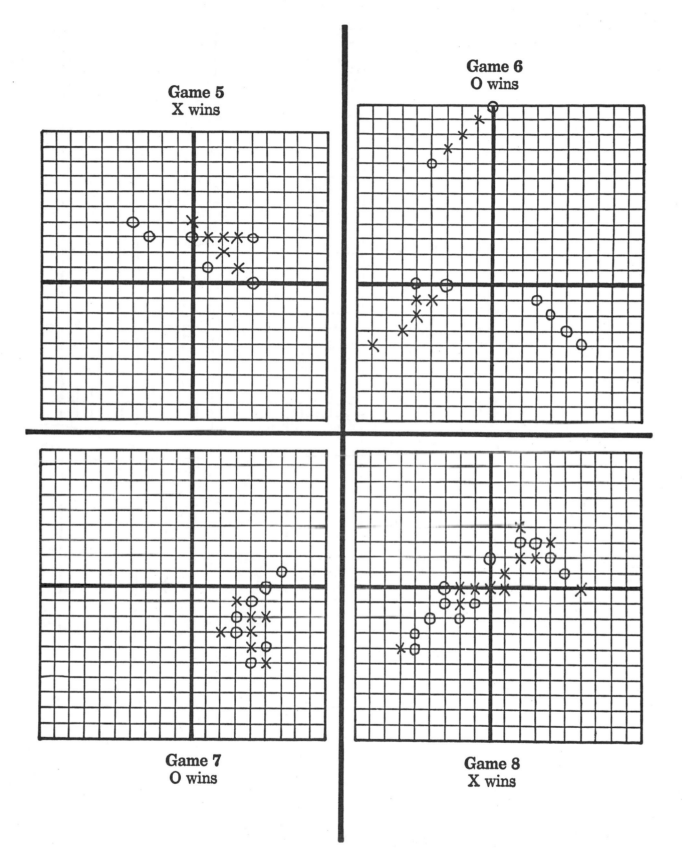

Game 5
X wins

Game 6
O wins

Game 7
O wins

Game 8
X wins

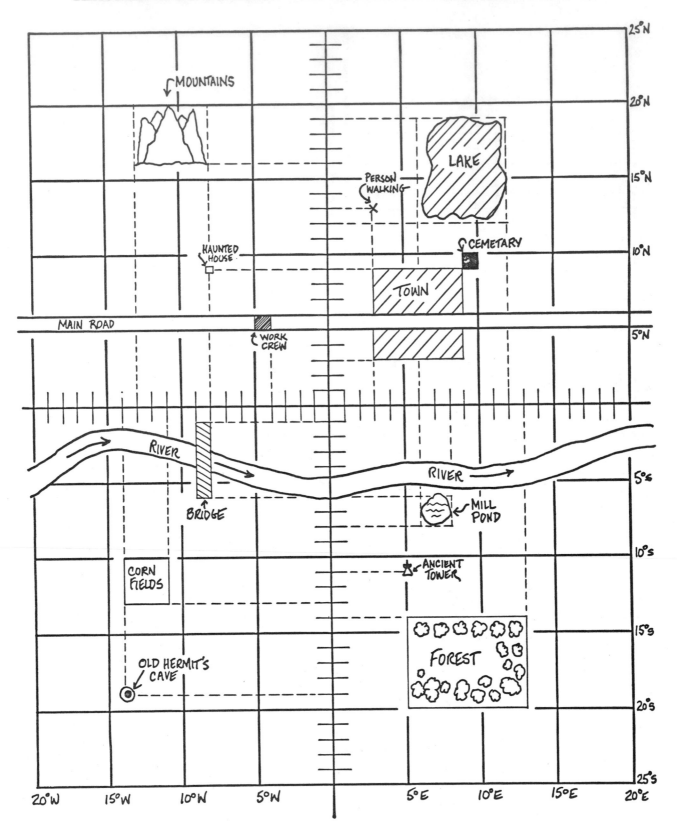

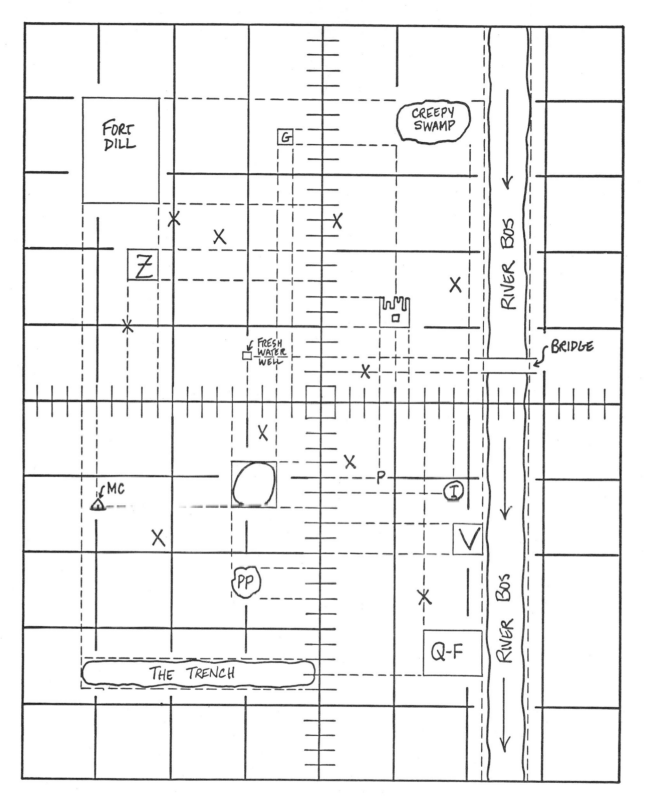

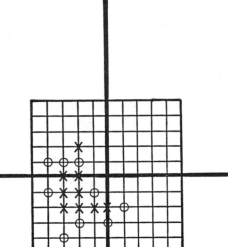

TEACHER ANSWER SHEET FOR GEOGRAPHY FINAL TEST:
PART III, MATCHING

1. Bay e
2. Continent s
3. Gulf i
4. Delta h
5. Isthmus q
6. Island c
7. Harbor b
8. Channel o
9. Canal n
10. River Source d
11. Oasis f
12. River Mouth a
13. Pass r
14. Sea m
15. Ocean l
16. Mountain Range g
17. Peninsula k
18. Reef j
19. Strait p
20. Longitude: Lines that run north and south and measure how far east or west you are of the prime meridian.
21. Latitude: Lines that run east and west and measure how far north or south you are of the equator.

HISTORICAL STUDY

Teacher Preview

Length of Project: 11 hours
Level of Independence: Intermediate
Goals:

1. To teach students how to choose a topic.
2. To introduce students to a variety of historical topics.
3. To produce a *Book of History*.
4. To require the use of research skills as students learn about specific topics.
5. To promote the concept of "kids teaching kids."
6. To place emphasis on independent learning.

During This Project Students Will:

1. Identify and choose topics.
2. Develop a list of research topics.
3. Choose historical periods that interest them.
4. Follow an outline to complete the project requirements.
5. Find facts and record them on notecards.
6. Prepare proper bibliographies.
7. Write correct research reports.
8. Write summaries of their reports to be included in the class's *Book of History*.
9. Make a presentation to the class.

Skills:

Preparing bibliographies	Accepting responsibility
Collecting data	Concentration
Library skills	Controlling behavior
Listening	Following project outlines
Making notecards	Individualized study habits
Summarizing	Persistence
Grammar	Time management
Handwriting	Personal motivation

Neatness

Paragraphs

Sentences

Spelling

Organizing

Setting objectives

Selecting topics

Divergent-convergent-evaluative thinking

Meeting deadlines

Self-awareness

Sense of quality

Setting personal goals

Creating presentation strategies

Public speaking

Self-confidence

Teaching others

Writing

Handouts Provided:

- "Choosing a Topic 1"
- "Choosing a Topic 2"
- "Choosing a Topic 3"
- "Student Assignment Sheet"
- Teacher's Introduction to the Student Research Guide (optional; see Appendix)
  a. "Notecard Evaluation"
  b. "Oral Presentation Evaluation"

- Student Research Guide (optional; see Appendix)
  a. "Bibliographies"
  b. "Notecards and Bibliographies"
  c. "Dewey Decimal Classification System"
  d. "The Card Catalog"
  e. *"Readers' Guide to Periodical Literature"*
  f. "Audio-Visual and Written Information Guides"
  g. "Where to Go or Write for Information"
  h. "Poster Display Sheet"
  i. "Things to Check Before Giving Your Presentation"
  j. "Visual Aids for the Oral Presentation"
  k. "Things to Remember When Presenting Your Project"
  l. "Daily Log"

PROJECT CALENDAR:

HOUR 1: _____ Students are assigned a historical period and work for the hour in the library. "Choosing a Topic 1" is used to record topic areas. HANDOUT PROVIDED	**HOUR 2:** _____ The hour is spent in the library as students work to complete the second handout on choosing a topic. HANDOUT PROVIDED	**HOUR 3:** _____ In class, topics for each historical period are written on the board, and they are discussed as possible research topics. HANDOUT PROVIDED
HOUR 4: _____ The research assignment is explained and students spend the hour in the library looking for topics they might like to study. HANDOUT PROVIDED STUDENTS TURN IN WORK	**HOUR 5:** _____ Students receive final topic approval and begin working on their research projects in the library. RETURN STUDENT WORK	**HOUR 6:** _____ Research work continues.
HOUR 7: _____ Research work continues.	**HOUR 8:** _____ In the classroom, students work on their presentations.	**HOUR 9:** _____ Students give their presentations.

PROJECT CALENDAR:

HOUR 10: _____	HOUR 11: _____	HOUR 12: _____
Students give their presentations.	Students receive their graded reports and the hour is used to discuss higher level thinking skills.	
STUDENTS TURN IN WORK	RETURN STUDENT WORK PREPARATION REQUIRED	

HOUR 13: _____	HOUR 14: _____	HOUR 15: _____

HOUR 16: _____	HOUR 17: _____	HOUR 18: _____

Lesson Plans and Notes

HOUR 1: Give students the "Choosing a Topic 1" handout. Assign each student one of the historical periods listed on the handout and have them spend the hour completing it in the library.

Notes:

- The first three handouts are provided to help students choose topics to study. The project can be conducted without these preliminary handouts; however, their use introduces students to a method for choosing a topic, which is an important skill.

- This project requires six hours of library time. If you have adequate reference materials (two sets of encyclopedias, minimum), these hours can be conducted in your classroom.

- Students are required to provide bibliographies for handouts 1 and 2. These bibliographies can be put on notecards with topic headings so that students can trade sources during Hour 4. It is important to emphasize to students that the historical period they are *assigned* in the first hour need not be the one they *choose* in the fourth hour.

- To produce a project that covers the greatest number of topics, devise a way of assigning historical periods to students: conduct a drawing, or select students one at a time and let them choose a period. Also, consider doing the project *twice,* first with each student doing a separate historical period, and the second time with the entire class concentrating on the same period.

- Working in a library is an independent undertaking. Spell out a code of conduct and rules of behavior clearly before setting students free. Also, spend some time explaining that research can sometimes be painstaking and that information is not always as readily available as we would like it to be.

- The handout for this hour asks students to find five "main" topics. This should be explained: main topics are broad and fairly general. They have lots of information available and can be easily broken down into a set of more specific subtopics.

HOUR 2: Give students the "Choosing a Topic 2" handout. The hour is spent in the library completing the handout.

HOUR 3: Give students the "Choosing a Topic 3" handout and have them fill it out as topics are discussed in class. Write the main topics that students worked with during Hour 2 for each historical period on the board as they are read and approved in class. At the end of the hour students put stars next to topics that are of most interest to them. Allow time for discussion and add an hour to your lesson plan if necessary.

HOUR 4: Give students the assignment sheet and explain the research project. Students spend the hour in the library choosing a historical period and possible topics to study. At the end of the hour each student hands in his or her choice of historical period, five possible topics, and a final topic choice.

Notes:

- You may want to require students to have a visual display with their presentations during Hours 9 and 10. If so, it should be assigned during this hour.
- Be sure to evaluate the topic choices that students make. Don't let anyone pursue a topic that has insufficient information available or that is frivolous in nature.

HOUR 5: Students receive final topic approval and begin working on their research projects in the library.

HOURS 6–8: Students work on their research and presentations.

HOUR 9: Students give their presentations.

HOUR 10: Students give their presentations. At the end of the hour each student hands in

1. Five bibliography cards
2. Twenty-five notecards
3. A three-page report
4. A one-page synopsis

HOUR 11: Return the graded reports to students and enter each synopsis that is adequately done into the *Book of History,* which you have prepared for this hour. Unsatisfactory work is rewritten and handed in at a later date. The remainder of this hour is designed to offer a discussion of higher level thinking skills, and how they were used during the project. The skills that are necessary for conducting a research project and presenting it to others are discussed: the ability to choose a topic, find, record, and interpret information, write a report, plan a presentation, and actually *teach* other people. Students who have gone through the experience of a research project such as this are prepared to tackle projects that allow even more independence.

Note:

- The assignment for this project is two-fold: students must write a three-page report and a one-page summary of the information obtained through research. The one-page summary is to be included in a *Book of History.* In its simplest form, this is a three-ring binder with divisions for each historical period listed on the student handout. The one-page summaries are filed in this book according to topic. The *Book of History* can be added to year after year.

General Notes About This Project:

- This project offers an excellent opportunity to require students to use the informational handouts, checklists and the "Daily Log" that are supplied in the Student Research Guide.

- Evaluation sheets for oral reports, posters, and notecards are provided in the "Teacher's Introduction to the Research Guide."

- This project idea works for a wide variety of subject areas, not just historical periods. It can be modified by adding periods to the list that is provided or it can be changed altogether by emphasizing a different subject.

Name _____ Date _____

HISTORICAL STUDY
Choosing a Topic 1

You will be assigned one of the historical periods listed below. Find five "main" (or "general") topics in library books that relate to this period of history. Don't list the first five topics you find, but try to include interesting or unusual topics; the kind *you* would like to study.

HISTORICAL PERIODS

1. Biblical times
2. Ancient Greece
3. The Times of Alexander the Great
4. The Roman Empire
5. The Dark Ages
6. The Middle Ages

7. The Renaissance
8. The Age of Exploration
9. The Industrial Revolution
10. The World Wars
11. Modern Times (since 1945)
12. The Space Age

Complete this handout during library research time. (Include a bibliography.)

Assigned historical period: _____

_____

Main Topic 1: _____

_____

Main Topic 2: _____

_____

Main Topic 3: _____

_____

Main Topic 4: _____

_____

Main Topic 5: _____

_____

Name _____ Date _____

HISTORICAL STUDY
Choosing a Topic 2

Every main topic can be further subdivided into more specific topics. For this assignment you will go back to the library to identify specific topics for each of the main topics you listed on handout 1. When you look up each of the main topics, you will discover other things that can be explored or studied. For example:

Historical period: _____ Roman Empire _____

    Main Topic 1. _____ Transportation _____

        Topic: _____ Chariots _____

        Topic: _____ Slave galleys (boats) _____

        Topic: _____ Road system _____

    Main Topic 2: _____ Government _____

        Topic: _____ Emperors _____

        Topic: _____ Senate _____

        Topic: _____ Laws _____

Name _____ Date _____

CHOOSING A TOPIC 2 (continued)

Fill out this handout during library research time, beginning with your main topics from handout 1. Include a bibliography.

Historical period: _____

Main Topic 1: _____

    Topic: _____

    Topic: _____

    Topic: _____

Main Topic 2: _____

    Topic: _____

    Topic: _____

    Topic: _____

Main Topic 3: _____

    Topic: _____

    Topic: _____

    Topic: _____

Main Topic 4: _____

    Topic: _____

    Topic: _____

    Topic: _____

Main Topic 5: _____

    Topic: _____

    Topic: _____

    Topic: _____

Bibliography:

Name _____ Date _____

HISTORICAL STUDY
Choosing a Topic 3

During this hour topics for each historical period will be listed on the board. When called upon, read the five *main* topics you have recorded on handout 1. Each main topic will be discussed before it is written on the board to decide if it would make a good research project. Be prepared to participate in the discussion: you may be asked to describe some of the 15 topics you found for handout 2. As main topics are written on the board, record them below. Try to decide for yourself if the topics listed would be suitable for research.

Remember that the work you did on handout 2 was designed to teach you how to identify specific topics. This will be a helpful skill as you begin working on the Historical Study.

BIBLICAL TIMES: *ANCIENT GREECE:*

1. _____   1. _____

2. _____   2. _____

3. _____   3. _____

4. _____   4. _____

5. _____   5. _____

6. _____   6. _____

7. _____   7. _____

8. _____   8. _____

9. _____   9. _____

10. _____   10. _____

CHOOSING A TOPIC 3 (continued)

THE TIMES OF ALEXANDER THE GREAT:

1. _____
2. _____
3. _____
4. _____
5. _____
6. _____
7. _____
8. _____
9. _____
10. _____

THE ROMAN EMPIRE:

1. _____
2. _____
3. _____
4. _____
5. _____
6. _____
7. _____
8. _____
9. _____
10. _____

THE DARK AGES:

1. _____
2. _____
3. _____
4. _____
5. _____
6. _____
7. _____
8. _____
9. _____
10. _____

THE MIDDLE AGES:

1. _____
2. _____
3. _____
4. _____
5. _____
6. _____
7. _____
8. _____
9. _____
10. _____

Name _____ Date _____

CHOOSING A TOPIC 3 (continued)

THE RENAISSANCE:

1. _____
2. _____
3. _____
4. _____
5. _____
6. _____
7. _____
8. _____
9. _____
10. _____

THE AGE OF EXPLORATION:

1. _____
2. _____
3. _____
4. _____
5. _____
6. _____
7. _____
8. _____
9. _____
10. _____

THE INDUSTRIAL REVOLUTION:

1. _____
2. _____
3. _____
4. _____
5. _____
6. _____
7. _____
8. _____
9. _____
10. _____

THE WORLD WARS:

1. _____
2. _____
3. _____
4. _____
5. _____
6. _____
7. _____
8. _____
9. _____
10. _____

CHOOSING A TOPIC 3 (continued)

MODERN TIMES (since 1945):   *THE SPACE AGE:*

1. _____   1. _____

2. _____   2. _____

3. _____   3. _____

4. _____   4. _____

5. _____   5. _____

6. _____   6. _____

7. _____   7. _____

8. _____   8. _____

9. _____   9. _____

10. _____   10. _____

To prepare for the next class, carefully review the list you have just finished. Put a mark next to each topic that you might be interested in learning more about.

Name _____ Date _____

HISTORICAL STUDY
Student Assignment Sheet

The ability to learn on your own opens new doors to learning possibilities because it allows you to choose topics to study. History is full of interesting stories and fascinating events, but information about them is stored in books, in people's experiences, and in a variety of other resources that might not easily be found. It takes a person who knows how to choose a topic, find information, record facts, and produce a final project to actually discover and learn about these stories and events.

For this project you will study a specific historical topic and present your findings to the class. You will then make your own personal contribution to the class's *Book of History*. The book is divided into the following general historical periods. You may choose any one of these periods for the project, and then you are free to choose a specific topic from this period to study.

1. Biblical Times
2. Ancient Greece
3. The Times of Alexander the Great
4. The Roman Empire
5. The Dark Ages
6. The Middle Ages
7. The Renaissance
8. The Age of Exploration
9. The Industrial Revolution
10. The World Wars
11. Modern Times (since 1945)
12. The Space Age

Here are the requirements for the historical study:

I. Choose a period in history to study.

II. After a little preliminary study about the period you have chosen *(this is important)*, select a topic that you want to research and learn about.

III. Find at least five sources of information about this topic. Each of these sources must be properly recorded on separate bibliography cards.

IV. Find at least twenty-five facts about the topic and record them on notecards.

V. Write a report about your topic. Include your twenty-five facts plus whatever other information you have gathered. It should be well written and neat: your best writing, please! This report should be at least three pages long.

VI. Develop a presentation to give to the class about your topic that teaches or illustrates your twenty-five facts in some way. The decision about the method of presentation is left up to you.

VII. Write a one-page summary of all the information you have obtained during this project. This summary will become a page in our class *Book of History*. Head the page with the historical period and the topic you have chosen. Your name and the date should appear on the second line. It can be no longer than *one page* and it should be an example of your very best writing. This is called a "synopsis of information."

List the choices you make for Historical Period and topics in the space below.

A. Historical Period: _____

HISTORICAL STUDY (continued)

B. Possible topics:

1. _____

2. _____

3. _____

4. _____

5. _____

C. Final Choice: _____

- -

Project Approval

_____ Your topic has been approved and you may begin research.

_____ I would like to discuss your topic choice with you before you begin research since it may need to be revised.

FAMOUS PEOPLE

Teacher Preview

Length of Project: 5 hours
Level of Independence: Intermediate
Goals:

1. To emphasize the use of research skills as students learn about famous people.
2. To allow students to write research reports in the form of biographies.

During This Project Students Will:

1. Choose a topic for a research project.
2. Prepare proper bibliography cards and notecards.
3. Assemble information for a report.
4. Write a biography.

Skills:

Preparing bibliographies	Organizing
Collecting data	Selecting topics
Library skills	Meeting deadlines
Listening	Accepting responsibility
Making notecards	Concentration
Summarizing	Controlling behavior
Grammar	Individualized study habits
Handwriting	Persistence
Neatness	Personal motivation
Paragraphs	Sense of quality
Sentences	Self-confidence
Spelling	Writing

Handouts Provided:

- "Student Assignment Sheet"
- Student Research Guide (optional; see Appendix)
  a. Choose handouts and checklists that fit your needs.

PROJECT CALENDAR:

HOUR 1:	HOUR 2:	HOUR 3:
Introduction to the project and discussion of famous people.	Students choose their own topics and begin conducting research in the library.	Library research continues.
HANDOUT PROVIDED PREPARATION REQUIRED		
HOUR 4:	**HOUR 5:**	**HOUR 6:**
Research is completed by the end of this hour. A due date is set for biographies to be turned in.	Biographies are turned in and the hour is spent discussing the usefulness of a research project in a social studies class.	
	STUDENTS TURN IN WORK	
HOUR 7:	**HOUR 8:**	**HOUR 9:**

Lesson Plans and Notes

HOUR 1: Give students the "Famous People Student Assignment Sheet." Spend the hour discussing famous people from each category on the handout, and develop a list on the board. Tell students that they must have their "Famous People" selections made by the beginning of the next hour.

> *Notes:*
>
> - This is a straightforward, simple research project that requires homework. Emphasis should be placed on accuracy, neatness, writing skills, topic selection, and the research process.
>
> - There are many famous people that students have probably never heard of. Make use of the first hour by coming to class prepared with a list of names that your students won't think of, but that would make good research topics.
>
> - For research purposes, it is best to have students choose famous people from at least five years ago or more. The further back in time a famous person lived, the more general sources of information will be available about him or her. Current famous people may be studied if information can be found.

HOURS 2–3: Students spend both hours in the library conducting research, preparing bibliography cards, and putting information on notecards.

> *Note:*
>
> - These two hours and Hour 4 are to be conducted in a library. The scope of the project is greatly restricted if library time cannot be provided. However, it is possible to do a biography project, on historical figures, entirely out of encyclopedias, and this could be done in a classroom. In this situation the requirement of finding five sources must be modified, unless other resources are available.

HOUR 4: Students complete their library research during this hour. Set a due date for completed biographies to be turned in.

HOUR 5: Have students turn in their completed biographies. Then spend the hour discussing the value of independent research and how the skills used for this project could be applied to other endeavors. Mention and discuss higher level thinking skills: to *learn,* one must be able to gain knowledge and comprehend what it means. To learn *independently,* one should be able to apply and analyze knowledge (or information). To *present* what has been learned independently to others by, for example, writing a biography of a famous person, one has to synthesize information from various sources into a final product. Help students recognize how a project like this prepares them for even more independent undertakings.

Name _____ Date _____

FAMOUS PEOPLE
Student Assignment Sheet

Studying history, to many people, is a dry, boring undertaking. That's because they don't see the human side of past events—the fact that people who had feelings, fears, and ambitions just like you have, did something with their lives that was significant. History is actually the study of *people,* and people are the most interesting subjects in the world! The key to studying interesting subjects like kings and explorers and scientists and sports heroes is the ability to learn on your own. Without it, you learn what you are told; with it, you choose your own subjects to investigate. Once a person has mastered the skills for independent learning, history becomes an almost endless list of interesting things to discover.

For this project you will select a famous person to study. This person should fit into one of the categories below. If you think of a famous person who does not fit one of these categories, get permission from your teacher to study him or her. Be sure there is information available about the person you choose.

1. Government leader
2. Religious leader
3. Adventurer/Explorer
4. Inventor
5. Doctor/Nurse/Researcher
6. Scientist
7. Soldier/Officer
8. Royalty
9. Athlete

10. Educator/Philosopher
11. Politician
12. Traitor/Spy
13. Entertainer
14. Business Person/Industrialist
15. Artist
16. Musician
17. Writer
18. Other _____

FAMOUS PEOPLE (continued)

Here is your assignment:

I.   Choose a famous person from one of the categories listed previously.
II. Find at least five sources of information and make a bibliography card for each source.
III. Find at least twenty-five facts about this famous person, and record them on notecards.
IV. Use your notecards to write a biography. This biography should be at least four pages long and include such things as

    A. Important dates (born, married, died; events)
    B. Husband's/wife's name
    C. Children
    D. Hometown
    E. Important events from the person's life (describe them briefly)
    F. What made the person famous
    G. What kinds of things were happening in the world while this person lived
    H. Other facts that you found in your research
    I. A character sketch (describe the person as best you can)
    J. Why you chose this person

V.   Hand in your *neatly* written biography along with five bibliography cards and twenty-five notecards on the date that is set in class.
VI. For this project:

    A. The name of the famous person I have chosen to study is:

    ———————————————————————————————

    B. My choice fits into this category (from the handout list):

    ———————————————————————————————

EARLY AMERICAN HISTORY

Teacher Preview

General Explanation:

This is a small group project (3 to 5 students per group) that emphasizes individual research and group cooperation as students design and create wall murals. A class of thirty students will produce six to ten murals for display. Each mural depicts people and events from one period in American history, based upon information gathered by group members through research.

Length of Project: 20 hours

Level of Independence: Advanced

Goals:

1. To help students investigate people, topics, and events from early American history.
2. To emphasize the use of research skills as students learn about specific topics.
3. To promote the concept of "kids teaching kids."
4. To place emphasis on independent learning.
5. To allow students to work together in small groups.

During This Project Students Will:

1. Work in small groups.
2. Select at least one person and one topic/event as subjects for an individual research project.
3. Follow an outline to complete the project requirements.
4. Assemble information for a report.
5. Create a mural.
6. Evaluate their projects.

Skills:

Preparing bibliographies
Collecting data
Library skills
Listening

Working with limited resources
Accepting responsibility
Concentration
Controlling behavior

Making notecards

Summarizing

Grammar

Handwriting

Neatness

Paragraphs

Sentences

Spelling

Group planning

Organizing

Setting objectives

Selecting topics

Divergent-convergent-evaluative thinking

Following and changing plans

Identifying problems

Meeting deadlines

Following project outlines

Individualized study habits

Persistence

Sharing space

Taking care of materials

Time management

Working with others

Personal motivation

Self-awareness

Sense of quality

Setting personal goals

Creative expression

Creating presentation strategies

Drawing/sketching/graphing

Poster making

Self-confidence

Teaching others

Handouts Provided:

- "Student Assignment Sheet"
- "Historical Period Roster"
- "Historical Period Topic Selection Sheet"
- "Student Self-Evaluation Sheet"
- "Final Evaluation"
- Student Research Guide (optional; see Appendix)
   a. Choose handouts and checklists that meet your needs.

PROJECT CALENDAR:

HOUR 1: _____ Introduction to the project. Students receive project handouts, and a time line for finishing project requirements is established. Students are assigned to their groups. HANDOUTS PROVIDED	**HOUR 2:** _____ Discussion of historical periods. Groups turn in their three top choices of historical periods to study. STUDENTS TURN IN WORK	**HOUR 3:** _____ Groups are assigned their historical periods. Students in each group begin working on historical "rosters" which were handed out during Hour 1.
HOUR 4: _____ Students continue working on rosters.	**HOUR 5:** _____ Rosters are completed by the end of the hour and handed in. STUDENTS TURN IN WORK	**HOUR 6:** _____ Rosters are returned. Each student chooses one person and one topic or event to study. These choices are handed in on "Topic Selection Sheets" which were handed out during Hour 1. RETURN STUDENT WORK STUDENTS TURN IN WORK
HOUR 7: _____ "Topic Selection Sheets" are returned. Students begin to study the topics they have chosen. Reference material must be available for Hours 7–14. RETURN STUDENT WORK	**HOUR 8:** _____ Students conduct research.	**HOUR 9:** _____ Students conduct research.

PROJECT CALENDAR:

HOUR 10: _____	HOUR 11: _____	HOUR 12: _____
Students conduct research.	Students conduct research.	Students conduct research. If they wish, they may begin writing reports during this hour.
HOUR 13: _____	**HOUR 14:** _____	**HOUR 15:** _____
Students conduct research and write reports.	Students conduct research and write reports.	Research papers, notecards and bibliographies are turned in. Groups meet and begin planning murals. STUDENTS TURN IN WORK
HOUR 16: _____	**HOUR 17:** _____	**HOUR 18:** _____
Students get their papers, notecards, and bibliographies back. Work on the murals is begun. RETURN STUDENT WORK NEED SPECIAL MATERIALS	Work on murals continues. NEED SPECIAL MATERIALS	Work on murals continues. NEED SPECIAL MATERIALS

PROJECT CALENDAR:

HOUR 19: _____	HOUR 20: _____	HOUR 21: _____
Work on murals continues; murals should be finished by the end of the hour. NEED SPECIAL MATERIALS	Murals are turned in. Students complete their self-evaluation forms and turn them in. A discussion of group dynamics and independent learning completes the project. HANDOUT PROVIDED STUDENTS TURN IN WORK	
HOUR 22: _____	**HOUR 23:** _____	**HOUR 24:** _____
HOUR 25: _____	**HOUR 26:** _____	**HOUR 27:** _____

Lesson Plans and Notes

HOUR 1: Introduce students to the entire project and its various components, and provide a time line to show when each part of the project is to be completed. Distribute and discuss all of the handouts, except the self-evaluation sheet. Small groups are then chosen, selected, appointed, assigned, or put together. (It is up to you to decide how to determine who is in each group.)

> *Note:*
>
> • This project offers an excellent opportunity to require students to use the handouts and checklists that are supplied in the Student Research Guide. Especially valuable is the "Daily Log," in which students keep track of their own progress. If these materials are to be used, they should be introduced during this hour.

HOUR 2: Spend the hour discussing the historical periods outlined in the "Early American History" assignment handout, adding whatever additional periods students can think of. During the final ten minutes of the hour each group produces a list of its members' top three choices for a period to study. This list is handed in.

HOUR 3: Tell students which historical period their group will study. (The method for making this determination is left to you.) Students then meet in small groups to develop "Historical Period Rosters." It is crucial that *plenty* of resource material be available at all times for this project, preferably right in your classroom. Encyclopedias serve as an excellent primary source. During this hour students identify people, topics, and events that were important during their group's period of history.

> *Notes:*
>
> • After groups have selected their historical periods (each group should have a *different* period), their first assignment is to create a "Historical Period Roster." This is more difficult than it sounds because there is no single resource that lists all of the people, topics, and events from colonial days, for instance. Often students must make educated guesses about certain people or topics and look them up to verify that they belong in a particular historical period. The search for one topic will likely yield clues to other topics. This can be time consuming and potentially frustrating if leads cannot be followed. To reduce frustration it is crucial that plenty of reference material be available.
>
> • Encourage students to help one another as they create their "Historical Period Rosters." If a student in one group finds a person who lived during a period that another group is studying, the information should be shared. If there are 30 investigators studying history books and encyclopedias and sharing information, the rosters will take shape quickly, and they will be fairly complete.

HOUR 4: Students continue to work on their rosters.

HOUR 5: Students finish their rosters by the end of the hour. No group should claim that it is "done" when time still remains. It is literally impossible to find and list all of the people, topics, and events from a major period of American history in three hours. Additional time can always be spent looking through another book or following new leads. Rosters are handed in at the end of this hour.

HOUR 6: Groups get their rosters back and each student decides on one person and one topic or event to study for research reports. Students meet in their small groups and topics are chosen after discussing what is needed to produce a quality mural. Group decision making plays a large role in each student's selection of a person and topic/event. At the end of this hour each group hands in a "Historical Period Topic Selection Sheet."

Notes:

- Students can assist one another here, also. For example, one student may say, "Is anyone studying Abraham Lincoln? I found a good book about him." You should encourage this kind of sharing, but be sure that each person is doing his or her own research.
- Be sure to evaluate the topic choices that your students make. Don't let anyone pursue a topic that has insufficient information available or that is frivolous in nature.

HOUR 7: "Topic Selection Sheets" are handed back and students begin to study the people and topics/events they have chosen. This information is recorded on notecards. Reference materials must be available for Hours 7–14.

HOURS 8–14: Students continue to study topics and write research papers. Research papers are to be complete and ready to hand in by the beginning of Hour 15.

HOUR 15: Research papers, notecards, and bibliographies are turned in at the beginning of the hour. Students then assemble in their groups to begin planning murals. At the end of the hour each group hands in a rough sketch of its mural, showing where each area of information will be located, and indicating other prominent features to be included. Graded materials are returned to students at the beginning of the next hour so they can be used for reference.

Note:

- Reports should be graded or checked before students begin to work on their murals. Be sure to allow enough time in your overall schedule to do a thorough job of grading for such things as accuracy, effort, neatness, and sufficient information. As much as a week may be needed between Hours 15 and 16.

HOURS 16–19: Students get their papers, notecards, and bibliographies back, and work in small groups on their murals until they are completed. A mural can accept infinite detail, so there is always something that can be added. When finished, the murals are displayed in the room or elsewhere in the school. Students are asked to evaluate themselves and their fellow group members in the general areas of cooperation, effort, quality of work, and organization/neatness.

You should evaluate students on a similar basis. The mural evaluation can be based on many different criteria. It is left to you to decide how to produce a final grade. (See the evaluation sheets provided in the "Teacher's Introduction to the Student Research Guide" for some ideas about evaluating student work.) There is also an "Early American History: Final Evaluation" provided at the end of this project.

> *Notes:*
>
> - Beginning with Hour 16, materials for making the murals must be available: mural paper, pencils, scissors, erasers, markers, watercolors, crayons, construction paper, and so forth.
> - You may want to include an oral presentation requirement with this project. If so, at least one additional hour will be necessary for groups to present their murals to the class.

HOUR 20: Murals are turned in at the beginning of the hour. Distribute the self-evaluation sheets and have students spend some time evaluating themselves and each member of their group. During the rest of the hour conduct a class discussion that focuses on how higher level thinking skills were applied during this project, especially at the synthesis level. Information was drawn from diverse places, processed by individuals into reports, and then organized on a mural according to a *plan*. Point out that most organizations and businesses deal with information in the same way the small groups did: individuals are given responsibilities and then each person's effort is blended into a final product. These are the key verbs to use when discussing synthesis:

> *Design*— students designed their own parts of the mural.
>
> *Plan*— the murals were planned by group discussion and consensus.
>
> *Create*— the murals were created from originally unconnected facts and the combined imaginations of the students.
>
> *Evaluate*— students evaluated their own work and the work of others in their group.

Name _____ Date _____

EARLY AMERICAN HISTORY
Student Assignment Sheet

The historic roots of the greatest superpower in the world lie in the stories of people and events from early American history. In a very short period of time (for a nation) America sprang from its infancy as thirteen tiny colonies clinging to the eastern shore of the North American continent, to full maturity as the most powerful country in the world. How did this dramatic rise to power occur? Who were the people who made it happen? What events led America to become a nation of strength and wealth? To answer these questions it is necessary to understand early American history, and independent study is one of the best ways to learn about it. Learning on your own allows you to choose topics of interest that may not be included in a regular history course. Because you have mastered key independent learning skills, you are allowed to decide for yourself what topic to investigate. This ability will be useful for the rest of your life.

This is a small-group *and* an individual project. As a group, you will select a period from early American history to study. Some suggestions are provided on this handout, but there are many more. Each group member will choose at least one event and one person to study individually as an independent research project. After each person has completed his or her individual research, the group will come back together to combine all of its information and create a wall mural.

Here is the "Early American History" assignment:

I. Your teacher will decide how to form small groups and how many members will be in each group.

II. You and your fellow group members will choose a period of early American history to study. Choose one of the periods listed below or find one on your own. If your group picks one that is not on the list, it must be okayed by the teacher. *Each group will study a different period,* so try to choose one that no other group is doing. Be prepared with two alternate choices in case your first choice is the same as another group's and you are asked to choose again. Here are some suggestions:

A. Native Americans before the twentieth century
B. Colonial days
C. Pioneers and the westward movement
D. The American Revolution
E. The industrial revolution
F. The "age of railroads"
G. The Spanish-American War
H. The term of any president from George Washington to Woodrow Wilson
I. The Civil War
J. World War I
K. The "gold rush"

1st Choice: _____

2nd Choice: _____

3rd Choice: _____

EARLY AMERICAN HISTORY (continued)

III. Gather as much information as possible about the period that has been approved for your group to study.

    A. List as many *people* as you can on the "Historical Period Roster."

    B. Identify *topics or events* on the "Historical Period Roster."

    C. Turn the completed roster in to be checked. It is due on this date:_____

IV. After the roster is returned, each group member will select one person and one topic/event from it to study. Record these choices on the "Historical Period Topic Selection Sheet" beside each member's name, and turn the sheet in for approval. It is due on this date:_____

V. Individual research

    A. Write a research report for each person and each topic or event that you study (minimum: one person and one topic/event).

        1. As you find information, record it on notecards, and refer your notecards to a bibliography. Notecards and bibliographies will be turned in with reports.

        2. Each written report must be at least two full pages long.

        3. Reports, notecards, and bibliographies are due on this date:_____

    B. You will begin the group project (creating a mural) when graded reports and notecards are handed back.

VI. Using information from each group member's reports, your group will design and create a wall mural.

    A. Make a small drawing of what the mural will look like, and turn it in to be checked. This is the mural plan and it will serve as a blueprint. The drawing is due on this date: _____

    B. When your group is satisfied with its plan, and it has been okayed by the teacher, begin working on the mural. Take your time and be careful: put as much quality into it as possible. *Sketch mural drawings in pencil before coloring them.*

    C. You will evaluate each other when the mural is finished. The evaluation will cover these areas:

        1. Total contribution to the project

        2. Sharing ideas

        3. Accepting others' ideas

        4. Concentrating on the project

        5. Taking care of materials

        6. Effort

        7. Willingness to work

        8. Quality of work

        9. General attitude

        10. Organization and neatness

VII. Your completed mural will be put on display in the classroom or somewhere else in the building. Each group member's name must be written on the front of the mural. The mural is due on this date:_____

Name _____ Date _____

HISTORICAL PERIOD ROSTER

YOUR GROUP'S HISTORICAL PERIOD: _____

GROUP MEMBERS: _____

_____

_____

_____

_____

   Identify and list people and events from your historical period, the more the better. This list will provide topic choices for the mural.

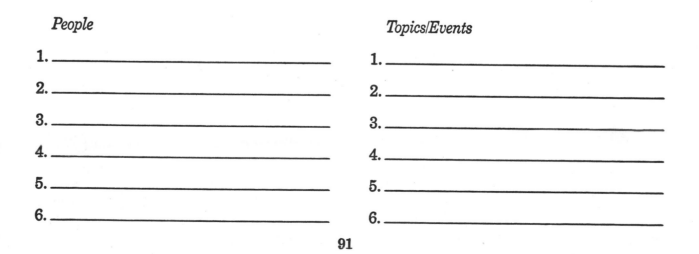

People

1. _____

2. _____

3. _____

4. _____

5. _____

6. _____

Topics/Events

1. _____

2. _____

3. _____

4. _____

5. _____

6. _____

HISTORICAL PERIOD ROSTER (continued)

People

7. _____
8. _____
9. _____
10. _____
11. _____
12. _____
13. _____
14. _____
15. _____
16. _____
17. _____
18. _____
19. _____
20. _____
21. _____
22. _____
23. _____
24. _____
25. _____

Topics/Events

7. _____
8. _____
9. _____
10. _____
11. _____
12. _____
13. _____
14. _____
15. _____
16. _____
17. _____
18. _____
19. _____
20. _____
21. _____
22. _____
23. _____
24. _____
25. _____

Name _____ Date _____

HISTORICAL PERIOD
TOPIC SELECTION SHEET

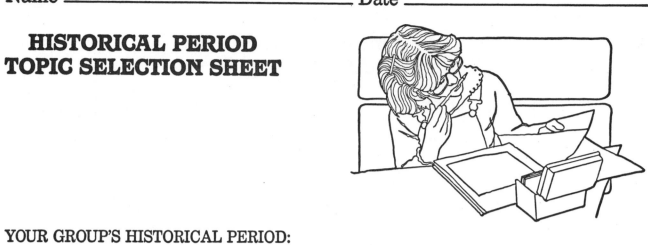

YOUR GROUP'S HISTORICAL PERIOD:

_____

Each person in the group will select one person and one topic or event from the "Historical Period Roster" and record them below. These are research topics and are to be studied independently. When research is completed, they will be represented on the mural by drawings and written information.

PEOPLE FROM HISTORY

Name of Person to Be Studied   *Student in Charge of Studying*

1. _____   _____

2. _____   _____

3. _____   _____

4. _____   _____

5. _____   _____

6. _____   _____

7. _____   _____

TOPICS AND EVENTS FROM HISTORY

Topic/Event to Be Studied   *Student in Charge of Studying*

1. _____   _____

2. _____   _____

3. _____   _____

4. _____   _____

5. _____   _____

6. _____   _____

7. _____   _____

Name _____ Date _____

EARLY AMERICAN HISTORY
Student Self-Evaluation Sheet

List the people in your group (including yourself) on the spaces across the top of this page. As fairly and honestly as you can, give each person an evaluation for the ten categories itemized in the left-hand column. Circle a number for each category under each group member's name: "1" is poor, "5" is excellent.

GROUP MEMBERS' NAMES

Evaluation Categories					
1. Total contribution to the project	1 2 3 4 5	1 2 3 4 5	1 2 3 4 5	1 2 3 4 5	1 2 3 4 5
2. Sharing ideas	1 2 3 4 5	1 2 3 4 5	1 2 3 4 5	1 2 3 4 5	1 2 3 4 5
3. Accepting others' ideas	1 2 3 4 5	1 2 3 4 5	1 2 3 4 5	1 2 3 4 5	1 2 3 4 5
4. Concentrating on the project	1 2 3 4 5	1 2 3 4 5	1 2 3 4 5	1 2 3 4 5	1 2 3 4 5
5. Taking care of materials	1 2 3 4 5	1 2 3 4 5	1 2 3 4 5	1 2 3 4 5	1 2 3 4 5
6. Effort	1 2 3 4 5	1 2 3 4 5	1 2 3 4 5	1 2 3 4 5	1 2 3 4 5
7. Willingness to work	1 2 3 4 5	1 2 3 4 5	1 2 3 4 5	1 2 3 4 5	1 2 3 4 5
8. Quality of work	1 2 3 4 5	1 2 3 4 5	1 2 3 4 5	1 2 3 4 5	1 2 3 4 5
9. General attitude	1 2 3 4 5	1 2 3 4 5	1 2 3 4 5	1 2 3 4 5	1 2 3 4 5
10. Organization and neatness	1 2 3 4 5	1 2 3 4 5	1 2 3 4 5	1 2 3 4 5	1 2 3 4 5
TOTAL (50 pts. possible)					

Name _____ Date _____

EARLY AMERICAN HISTORY
Final Evaluation

I. Historical Person: _____

    A. Bibliography   5 pts._____

    B. Notecards   5 pts._____

    C. Report

        1. Grammar, spelling, paragraphs, etc.   5 pts._____

        2. Content (appropriate information)   5 pts._____

        3. Neat, easy-to-understand, and written in your own words   5 pts._____

        4. Effort   5 pts._____

II. Historical Topic/Event: _____

    A. Bibliography   5 pts._____

    B. Notecards   5 pts._____

    C. Report

        1. Grammar, spelling, paragraphs, etc.   5 pts._____

        2. Content (appropriate information)   5 pts._____

        3. Neat, easy-to-understand, and written in your own words   5 pts._____

        4. Effort   5 pts._____

III. Mural (Historical Period: _____)

    A. Working with others   10 pts._____

    B. Contribution to the finished mural   10 pts._____

    C. Taking care of materials   5 pts._____

    D. Effort   5 pts._____

    E. Neatness   5 pts._____

    F. Idea sharing and willingness to compromise   5 pts._____

                                           (100 possible)   TOTAL_____

Comments:

INDIVIDUALIZED LEARNING PROJECTS
Teacher Preview

Project Topics:

The American Civil War
American Presidents
The American Revolution
Ancient Cultures and Civilizations
Birth of a Superpower: The Russian Revolution
Black History
Career Exploration
Current Events Bulletin Board
Current News Scrapbook
Economics: Prices Now and Then
The Great Depression
Historic Figures
Letter to the Editor
My Home State
My Neighborhood
The Vietnam War
Women in History
World War II

Length of Each Project:

1. 3 classroom hours (plus)
2. 3 weeks of students' own time

Level of Independence: Advanced

Goals:

1. To encourage the proper use of research skills as students learn about specific social studies topics.
2. To emphasize individualized learning.
3. To promote the concept of "kids teaching kids."

4. To provide a wide variety of subjects and topics for students to study.

5. To offer an opportunity for accelerated learners to work beyond the scope of the regular curriculum.

During This Project Students Will:

1. Choose a topic for independent study.

2. Complete a contract that describes a social studies research project.

3. Use independent learning skills to assemble information for a report/presentation/display.

4. Make a final presentation to the teacher, the class or some other audience.

Skills:

Preparing bibliographies
Collecting data
Library skills
Listening
Making notecards
Observing
Summarizing
Grammar
Handwriting
Neatness
Paragraphs
Sentences
Spelling
Organizing
Outlining
Setting objectives
Selecting topics
Divergent-convergent-evaluative thinking
Following and changing plans
Identifying problems
Meeting deadlines
Working with limited resources

Accepting responsibility
Concentration
Controlling behavior
Following project outlines
Individualized study habits
Persistence
Sharing space
Taking care of materials
Time management
Personal motivation
Self-awareness
Sense of quality
Setting personal goals
Creative expression
Creating presentation strategies
Diorama and model building
Drawing/sketching/graphing
Poster making
Public speaking
Self-confidence
Teaching others
Writing

Handouts Provided:

● "Individualized Project Study Packet"

● "Individualized Project Contract"

- "Individualized Learning Mid-Project Report Sheet"
- "Individualized Project Self-Evaluation Sheet"
- "Student Assignment Sheet" for each area of study
- Student Research Guide (see Appendix)

PROJECT CALENDAR:

HOUR 1: _____	HOUR 2: _____	HOUR 3: _____
Students are introduced to the list of available topics and the procedures for conducting an individualized learning project are explained.	Students receive assignment sheets for their top three project choices. After studying them, students select the one project they want to work on and return the other two. Projects are done on students' own time.	Projects are presented and self-evaluation sheets, which were handed out during Hour 1, are completed.
HANDOUTS PROVIDED	HANDOUTS PROVIDED	STUDENTS TURN IN WORK
HOUR 4: _____	HOUR 5: _____	HOUR 6: _____
HOUR 7: _____	HOUR 8: _____	HOUR 9: _____

Lesson Plans and Notes

HOUR 1: Introduce students to the project, and discuss the topics that are available. If the study packet, contract, mid-project report sheet, and self-evaluation sheet are to be used, hand these out and discuss them. Tell students they are to be ready to choose three project titles that sound interesting at the beginning of the next hour. They will read the assignment sheets for all three projects and then select one to work on. You may want to provide each student with a special notebook or folder to store their handouts and materials in. Since this is an advanced independent project, students can be expected to be responsible for keeping their materials in order.

Notes:

- Following this teacher preview is a set of materials that are designed to help students work on their own. These handouts are optional, and may be used to whatever extent is desired. Briefly, here is an explanation of what they are.

INDIVIDUALIZED STUDY PACKET: This handout offers helpful advice and suggestions about: choosing a topic, conducting research, writing a report, preparing an oral report, preparing a visual display (posters, mobiles, collages, murals, dioramas, photography, and other possibilities) and making a final presentation.

INDIVIDUALIZED PROJECT CONTRACT: Each of the projects is written to correspond with a standard learning contract that should be filled out before the project is approved. The contract requires a student to identify ten specific topics, choose one to study, and locate at least five sources of information about the chosen topic. This preliminary work helps ensure a project that can be successfully completed. The contract can be used to help students get started on their projects and to keep track of individual workloads. A learning contract tends to legitimize the work students are required to do, and it gives their efforts an added importance.

INDIVIDUALIZED LEARNING MID-PROJECT REPORT SHEET: The mid-project report is a tool for helping students maintain momentum, analyze their progress, and provide you with a record of their work. It requires students to write down what they have accomplished at the midpoint of their projects and it asks them to identify problems, roadblocks, and unforeseen obstacles that they have encountered.

INDIVIDUALIZED PROJECT SELF-EVALUATION SHEET: You may want to get your students' insights into their own work. If so, a self-evaluation sheet is included for this purpose. Self-evaluation is an important component of independent study, and it is a good way of introducing students to the concept of evaluating their efforts in these areas: individualized study habits, following the contract and project outline, accurate mid-project report, written report, visual display, and oral presentation. There is also space on the self-evaluation sheet for student and teacher comments.

- A list of the projects that are available for study should be provided during this hour. This can be simply a list of titles, or it can be a set of brief synopses that describe the projects. Remember that the list can be gradually expanded by developing new projects, based on the model that is provided here.

- If you use the contract, it should be given to students *before* they choose a project to work on. The contract instructs students to ask for a list of projects that are available to them. There are eighteen individualized projects in this book and you can add more if you wish. The contract instructs each student to find three projects that sound interesting, record the titles on the contract, and then ask the teacher for *all three* handouts to examine. After reading each handout, the student selects a project to work on and returns the remaining two handouts. The rest of the contract—identifying topics and finding sources—is then completed. A contract is not signed until ten specific topics have been identified and one of them has been chosen for the project. Five sources of information about this topic must also be recorded. The preliminary work required by the contract ensures that only those students who are truly motivated will commit themselves to a signed contract. It also encourages students to do some research before actually starting the project: it introduces them to the subject.

HOUR 2: Students come to class prepared with their top three project choices. Give students the assignment sheets for all three and have them spend the hour reading them and deciding which one to pursue. When they have decided on one, the other two assignment sheets are returned. Then instruct students to fill out contracts within the next few days. As soon as you approve their contracts, students can begin working on their individualized projects. If the mid-project report is being used, set a date for it to be turned in. Also, set a due date for submission of the final project. Have students record these dates on their contracts.

Notes:

- Each of the projects is self-explanatory, but *the handouts are brief and make the assumption that the students who are using them have previous experience working from project outlines.* The projects are designed to allow students to decide such things as how they will record information, the types of information sources they will use as well as their methods of presentation and the style of their reports.

- Students should be told not to write their names or anything else on a project handout until their contract is signed. When a student returns two of the three project assignment sheets that were checked out for examination, they should be clean and ready for someone else to look at. To help discourage writing on the handouts, no place for names or dates has been put on them.

HOUR 3: Students bring their finished projects to class and present or display them. Have students evaluate their own work by filling out the self-evaluation sheets that were distributed during Hour 1.

General Notes About This Project:

- The 18 projects that are provided in this section of the book can be used in many ways. The contract, mid-project report, and self-evaluation sheet are optional; each project stands on its own and can be used as it is with students who have the skills to learn on their own. You may wish to alter or rewrite project outlines to meet your own needs: they can be used as totally independent projects that are done at home, as individualized projects that are done in the classroom, or as small-group or full-group projects that are worked on as a class. You also have the option of creating entirely new projects, based on the model that is provided here.

- It is important to emphasize bibliographies as a necessary part of independent research; students should understand their responsibility for proving the accuracy of their research data and appreciate the value of authoritative information. The names of people who are interviewed should be recorded, along with their titles, occupations, or some other indication of why they are qualified to talk about a particular topic. Television shows that provide information should also be recorded: name of the program, the producer, the network or station that broadcast the program, and the date and time that it aired. The bibliographies for these projects can include more than five sources—the more the better! Although the contract calls for five sources of information before a project may be started this should not be considered the end of research; more sources can usually be found.

- There will be occasions when students choose topics that do not have five good sources of information available. They should be allowed to proceed *with your permission.* Be sure to pursue all avenues before conceding that five sources are not available.

- Most of the project handouts do not require written reports. Instead, they have this basic requirement: "Design a presentation that explains what you have learned." If a writing requirement is to be included (which is not a bad idea), inform your students, and tell them what is expected in a written report. The "Individualized Project Self-Evaluation Sheet" includes a section in which students evaluate their written work. If a report is not required, have students use this section to evaluate their written material on posters and other visual displays.

- In the "Individualized Project Study Packet" students are told to refer to the Student Research Guide for help. Be sure to make this valuable resource (found in the Appendix) available to your students.

Name _____ Date _____

INDIVIDUALIZED PROJECT STUDY PACKET

This packet includes suggestions about:
I. Choosing a topic
II. Conducting research
III. Writing a report
IV. Preparing an oral report
V. Visual displays
VI. Final presentations

Individualized projects are designed to let you take charge of your own learning. The *process of learning* is just as important as the information learned from projects like these. Your interests and the things you want to learn about will change from year to year, but the process for learning about them remains the same regardless of how old you are. Successfully completing an individualized project sets the stage for a lifetime of independent learning. The skills that are necessary for the project you are beginning today are the same skills used in high school, college, business, science, and everywhere else in the world where people are learning about things that interest them. If you can master these skills at your age, the future holds many bright and mysterious promises: you will be able to learn about anything you want!

This study packet is an outline filled with hints about conducting an individualized project. These are not assignments: they are *suggestions for completing the requirements* of projects that help you learn on your own.

I. CHOOSING A TOPIC

    A. Choose a topic that is specific enough to be covered adequately in a report. If you select a general topic, like the Civil War, give it a specific subtitle, like "Important Generals" or "Major Battles." A more specific topic would be "General Robert E. Lee" or "The Battle of Gettysburg." The important point here is that a report should supply what its title promises. If you title it "The Civil War," you are biting off more than you can chew. No single report can cover all of the Civil War.

    B. On the other hand, be careful about becoming too specific. The reason is simple: you have to work within the limits of your resources. An extremely specific topic requires special references that may not be accessible. For example, a topic such as "The Musical Preferences of U.S. Grant," greatly reduces the number of references and amount of material available for the project.

    C. When choosing a topic, it makes sense to list as many topics as possible, choose three or four that are most appealing, and then choose the one that seems best or most interesting.

II. CONDUCTING RESEARCH

A. You should already be able to use the library on your own. In addition, research can be conducted by interviewing, letter writing, using the telephone, using a computer, and finding information at home in newspapers and periodicals. When in the library, be sure to make use of encyclopedias, the card catalog, the microfilm library, *Readers' Guides to Periodical Literature,* biographies and autobiographies, vertical files, special reference materials, and the librarians themselves.

B. Record information on notecards, one fact per card. This allows you to arrange and rearrange facts before you write a report or arrange them on a visual display.

C. Keep a complete bibliography as you gather information.

D. Use the Student Research Guide to help answer questions about research.

III. WRITING A REPORT

A. Outline the report before writing it: put notecards in the order that you want information presented, and then make an outline that shows what will be in each paragraph of the report.

B. Write a rough draft of the report and ask someone (a teacher, parent, or older brother or sister) to proofread it, marking mistakes and making comments.

C. Rewrite the rough draft into a final report. Keep in mind that grammar, spelling, punctuation, capitalization, sentences, paragraphs, and neatness are all important quality factors.

IV. PREPARING AN ORAL REPORT

A. The most important advice: be familiar with your material. Study your report carefully and review all of the facts before giving a presentation. Don't present any facts that you don't understand: if you're not sure, find out!

B. Use the checklists in the Student Research Guide as an aid in preparing your report and presentation.

C. Remember that posture, eye contact, voice projection, and use of hands are important components of a good presentation.

D. Be familiar with your visual display so that examples can be quickly pointed out and discussed.

E. Be prepared to answer questions from the class following the presentation.

F. Understand this point clearly: the purpose of an oral presentation is to *teach* others about what has been learned. Design your presentation so that others will learn from what you have to say.

V. PREPARING A VISUAL DISPLAY

A. A visual display should exhibit some of the important facts and information from a report. It should be designed so that people can learn from it just by looking at it, even if you are not there to explain it.

B. Neatness, accuracy, informativeness, and originality are all important components of a visual display.

C. There are several kinds of visual displays that can be produced. Remember that artistic appeal is important, but presentation of information is the *purpose* of a visual display.

1. *POSTERS:* This is the most common form of display. Use parallel lines for all lettering, and be sure that drawings, articles, pictures, and other printed materials are neatly trimmed and arranged symmetrically on the posterboard. Use your own printing and lettering instead of stencils, and avoid using different colors for different letters in the headings and captions. A poster should contain at least one original drawing, and information and facts written in your own words. Don't just fill up a posterboard with magazine articles and newspaper headlines.

2. *MOBILES:* Mobiles are essentially a grouping of artistic mini-posters. Be sure that the concept for your mobile is workable: use cardboard cutouts and experiment with their arrangement to ensure that the mobile hangs correctly. Once a good mobile design is developed, do the same things you would for a poster. Remember that both sides of a mobile piece can be seen, so information should appear on both sides of every piece.

3. *COLLAGES:* A collage is less orderly than a poster, but it should be informative nonetheless. *Carefully* lay out the collage before writing or pasting anything. A collage should contain samples of your own writing and drawing as well as pictures, headlines, and articles from magazines and newspapers. A person should be able to learn about your topic by studying the collage: it should display facts and important points that will be made in an oral presentation.

4. *MURALS:* Murals are fun to create, and they can add a lot to a presentation. Be careful, though: a good mural is difficult to make. A mural is more than a collage because it shows *relationships* between people and events. A collage is an attractive way of presenting facts, without necessarily relating them; a mural shows how the facts combine or build upon one another. A mural tells a story. For example, a mural could be used to explain the events that led to the Battle of Gettysburg, or it could illustrate the battlefield as a map, showing where each army unit was located at the beginning of the fight, with arrows pointing out various movements during the battle. The possibilities are endless for using murals as visual displays of social studies topics.

5. *DIORAMAS:* Dioramas are three-dimensional models of specific scenes, such as Abraham Lincoln delivering the Gettysburg Address. To undertake a diorama, you must obtain permission from your teacher. A diorama can be useful if it shows an important event or moment from history. The easiest kind to make is a "shoebox diorama" (built inside a shoebox) with cardboard standups for human characters, props built from cardboard, toothpicks, Popsicle sticks, construction paper, and other common materials, and backgrounds drawn with ink and markers on plain white or colored paper. A brief written explanation should always accompany a diorama so that the viewer knows exactly what is being illustrated.

6. *PHOTOGRAPHY:* You may own a camera or have access to one at home or at school. If so, a photographic display is an option to consider. Take pictures of places in your community, historic sites that you visit on vacations or field trips, artifacts or exhibits at a museum, your own drawings and illustrations, pictures out of books and magazines, news headlines, models, and a multitude of other things that illustrate your social studies topic. Have the photographic negatives made into prints and design a bulletin board display, mount the photographs on posterboard, make a photo album or produce a "scrapbook." Or, take slides and organize a slideshow to go with your presentation. You should be able to talk about each picture, or write a caption for each one, to explain what is being illustrated.

7. *OTHER VISUAL DISPLAY POSSIBILITIES:*
   a. A dramatization or brief play
   b. A puppet play
   c. A computer program or demonstration
   d. A computer printout
   e. A display of artifacts, specimens, or documents
   f. A display of your own drawings
   g. A demonstration

VI. GIVING YOUR FINAL PRESENTATION

There is plenty of advice and instruction for presenting projects in the Student Research Guide. The most important ingredients for a quality presentation are

A. Plenty of research
B. Proper preparation
C. Practice
D. Self-confidence

Difficulties will undoubtedly arise during the course of an individualized project. There are always unexpected problems that must be overcome. Remember that students generally are not allowed to work independently unless they are capable of accepting responsibility and overcoming problems. The true test of independence is a person's ability to decide what to do when a plan runs into a roadblock. This is where many people quit, because they think that most problems are unsolvable and that if a plan doesn't work on the first try it is a failure. Always keep this in mind: nobody is perfect, including you. Your project may not be the best in the world, but it is *your own work!* If problems develop, do your best to solve them and keep forging ahead. *Be persistent!* If a plan doesn't work right, *don't give up!* Make a new plan and continue working. Have confidence! *The most important goal in an individualized project is to finish what is started, to fulfill the responsibility of completing a job.* A project may not be as good as it seemed it would be when first planned, and it definitely will not be perfect, but it is your very own work and that is what makes it special. By working hard, much can be learned about the *process of learning,* which should be your primary objective. This will ensure that the *next* project will be even better.

Name _____ Date _____

INDIVIDUALIZED PROJECT CONTRACT

When you become involved in an individualized learning project it is assumed that you are willing to work independently to complete it. A signed contract indicates your willingness to accept such a responsibility. Put some time and effort into this contract before turning it in for approval. It is the teacher's record of what you are doing and it is proof that you are serious about undertaking a specific project. Fill the contract out *completely* and sign on the line marked "Student Signature," then hand it in. The teacher will decide if you will be allowed to work on the project, based on grades, behavior, and performance in class. If you qualify to work on an individualized project, the contract will be signed by the teacher and a copy of it will be returned to you.

I. Ask for a list of individualized projects that are available to work on. Study the list carefully, and then request an assignment sheet for each of your three favorite project titles. List these three projects here:

   A. _____

   B. _____

   C. _____

II. Choose the project of greatest interest and record its title below. This will become your individualized project if the teacher signs the contract. Keep the assignment sheet for the project you have chosen, and return the other two.

PROJECT TITLE: _____

Subtitle (if any): _____

© 1987 by The Center for Applied Research in Education, Inc.

Name _____ Date _____

INDIVIDUALIZED PROJECT CONTRACT (continued)

III. Following the instructions on the project assignment sheet, identify ten topics that could be studied for this project. Be as specific as possible. *Be sure to read your assignment sheet before making this list!* Some handouts provide topic suggestions to help you get started.

A. _____

B. _____

C. _____

D. _____

E. _____

F. _____

G. _____

H. _____

I. _____

J. _____

IV. Choose the *topic* (from the list above) that you want to study and record it here:

TOPIC: _____

V. Find five sources of information about this topic *before* beginning the project. Only two of these sources can be encyclopedias; the others can be books, magazines, newspapers, or other credible sources. List five sources below, just as you would record a bibliography, to show that there is adequate information available about the topic you have chosen.

A. _____

_____

B. _____

_____

C. _____

_____

D. _____

_____

E. _____

_____

Name _____ Date _____

INDIVIDUALIZED PROJECT CONTRACT (continued)

VI. Sign this contract, then hand it to your teacher for approval.

I, _____ , agree to complete
(Your name)

this project to the best of my ability. I have chosen a topic that interests me and I am willing to work on my own to produce a quality project.

_____   _____
(Student Signature)   (Date)

- -

_____ has completed all
(Print student's name)

assignments, is passing all subjects, continues to do satisfactory work, and is allowed to begin an individualized project titled:

_____
(Print project title)

_____   _____
(Teacher Signature)   (Date)

Mid-Project Report Sheet Due Date: _____

Final Project Due Date: _____

Name _____ Date _____

INDIVIDUALIZED LEARNING
MID-PROJECT REPORT SHEET

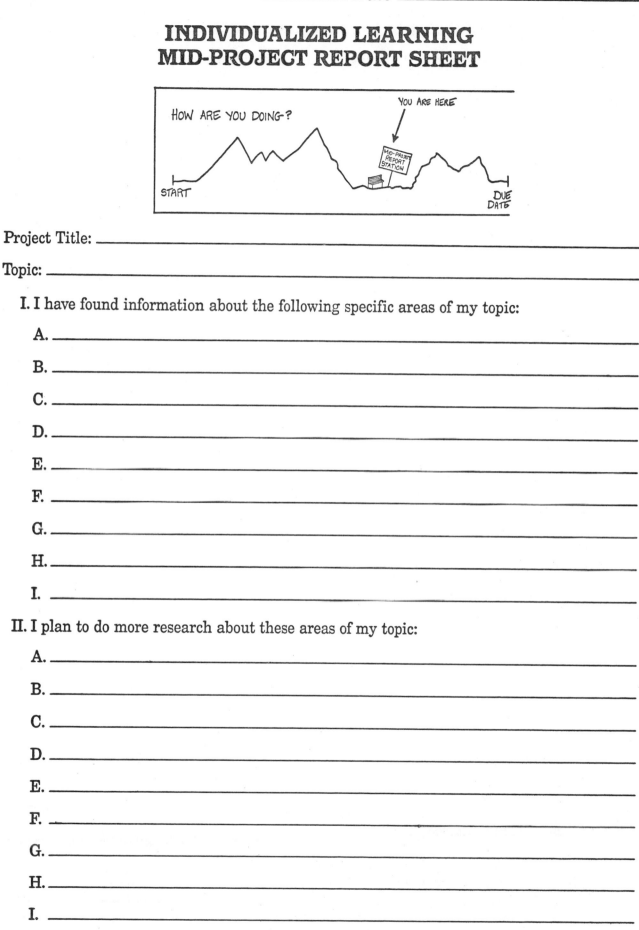

Project Title: _____

Topic: _____

I. I have found information about the following specific areas of my topic:

A. _____

B. _____

C. _____

D. _____

E. _____

F. _____

G. _____

H. _____

I. _____

II. I plan to do more research about these areas of my topic:

A. _____

B. _____

C. _____

D. _____

E. _____

F. _____

G. _____

H. _____

I. _____

Name _____ Date _____

INDIVIDUALIZED LEARNING MID-PROJECT REPORT SHEET (continued)

III. I have decided what my visual display will look like. (Mark one.)

    A. Yes _____

    B. No _____

    C. If you marked yes, describe what your visual display will look like; attach a drawing if it will help.

    _____

    _____

    _____

IV. Specific information about my project to date:

    A. I have completed _____ notecards. (Record how many.)

    B. I have used _____ sources of information. (Record how many.)

    C. Bibliography of sources I have taken information from:

        1. _____

        2. _____

        3. _____

        4. _____

        5. _____

V. Problem solving

    A. I have had difficulty finding information about these areas of my topic:

        1. _____

        2. _____

        3. _____

    B. I am having difficulties in the following areas (check each one that applies):

      _____ 1. Finding information.

      _____ 2. Making notecards and preparing a bibliography.

      _____ 3. Finding enough time to work on my project.

      _____ 4. Designing a visual display.

      _____ 5. Planning a presentation.

      _____ 6. Organizing my material for a written report.

      _____ 7. Understanding the information I've found (too technical, too detailed, too difficult, too much).

      _____ 8. Deciding what information to use and what *not* to use.

      _____ 9. Disciplining myself to work on my own.

      _____10. I am not having any problems: my project is going smoothly.

      _____11. Other. Explain: _____

Name _____ Date _____

INDIVIDUALIZED LEARNING MID-PROJECT REPORT SHEET (continued)

VI. I have found at least five things that I want to teach during my presentation. They are

A. _____

B. _____

C. _____

D. _____

E. _____

VII. Do you need any help or advice from the teacher before you continue with the project?

A. Yes _____

B. No _____

C. If you marked yes, explain what kind of help you need:

1. _____

_____

2. _____

_____

3. _____

_____

- -

Please check the statement that applies and sign this form before handing it in.

_____ I believe my work is progressing and I am confident that I can complete this project to my own satisfaction by its due date of _____.
                                                            (Due date)

_____ At this point, I am having so many problems with my project that I don't know if I can complete it by its due date of _____
                                                            (Due date)

Student Signature: _____

- -

TEACHER COMMENTS:

Name _____ Date _____

INDIVIDUALIZED PROJECT SELF-EVALUATION SHEET

At the conclusion of an individualized project there is only one person who really knows if you have done your best work. That person, of course, is *you!* The final step in an individualized project is to evaluate yourself and what you produced. Your own definition of "quality" and "effort" will determine how you evaluate your performance in the following areas.

I. Individualized Study Habits (those times when you worked on your project away from school, on your own)

   A. Evaluate how well you concentrated on the project. _____ (0–5 pts.)

   B. Evaluate how well you took care of materials and kept the work area clean. _____ (0–5 pts.)

   C. Evaluate the amount of time you set aside for this project: "0" is not nearly enough time, and "5" is plenty of time. _____ (0–5 pts.)

   D. Evaluate your attitude and behavior as you worked on this project. _____ (0–5 pts.)

                                                   SUBTOTAL _____ (20 pts. possible)

II. Following the Contract and Project Outline

   A. Give yourself from 0–5 points, depending on how "intelligent" you were about selecting a topic to study. _____ (0–5 pts.)

   B. Evaluate your persistence in looking for information. Did you find and use most of the sources that were available? _____ (0–5 pts.)

   C. Evaluate your notecards. Did you produce enough and are they written properly? _____ (0–5 pts.)

   D. Evaluate your bibliography. Is it complete and properly written? _____ (0–5 pts.)

   E. Give yourself from 0–10 points, depending on how much effort you put into your project. _____ (0–10 pts.)

                                                   SUBTOTAL _____ (30 pts. possible)

III. Accurate Mid-Project Report

   A. Give yourself from 0–5 points, depending on how much effort you put into completing the mid-project report. _____ (0–5 pts.)

   B. Evaluate the accuracy of your mid-project report. Was it an honest and correct record of your progress on the project up to that time? _____ (0–5 pts.)

                                                   SUBTOTAL _____ (10 pts. possible)

Name _____ Date _____

INDIVIDUALIZED PROJECT SELF-EVALUATION SHEET (continued)

IV. Written Report

    A. Evaluate how complete your report is: does it cover the topic thoroughly and include all of the important facts you found? _____ (0–5 pts.)

    B. Evaluate the report's neatness and basic appearance: spelling, grammar, sentences and paragraphs. _____ (0–5 pts.)

    C. Evaluate your report's accuracy. Are you sure of all the facts? _____ (0–5 pts.)

                  SUBTOTAL _____ (15 pts. possible)

V. Visual Display

    A. Evaluate the neatness of your display: drawings, pictures, clippings, and writing. _____ (0–5 pts.)

    B. Evaluate how well your display presents facts and information about the topic: Is the information accurate? Does your bibliography cover all the facts? Are facts presented clearly? _____ (0–5 pts.)

    C. Give yourself from 0–5 points, depending on how close you think the display is to being the best work you are capable of. _____ (0–5 pts.)

                  SUBTOTAL _____ (15 pts. possible)

VI. Oral Presentation

    A. Evaluate your presentation mechanics: eye contact, voice projection, speaking style, use of hands, use of visual display materials, and so forth. _____ (0–5 pts.)

    B. Evaluate how well you *taught* your audience about the topic. Did you present facts and information so that others could understand them? _____ (0–5 pts.)

                  SUBTOTAL _____ (10 pts. possible)

                 FINAL SCORE _____ (100 pts. possible)

STUDENT COMMENTS:

TEACHER COMMENTS:

THE AMERICAN CIVIL WAR
Student Assignment Sheet

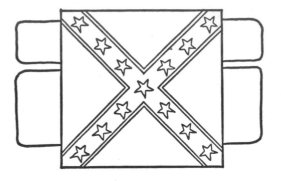

I. INTRODUCTION

A "civil war" occurs when the people within a single country have such differing views about how they should be governed or how they should live that they fight a war to decide. The side that wins the war establishes the lifestyle and the kind of government it wants. Civil wars can happen because of economics, religion, issues of freedom, unequal wealth distribution, tyranny, cultural disagreements, and racial or ethnic conflicts.

The American Civil War was a terrible chapter in the pages of history. It was the first truly mechanized war in the history of the world, with the use of railroad transportation, mass-produced guns, and metal ships. The reasons for the Civil War were complex, but slavery and the rights of individual states were key elements. The South, led by Jefferson Davis, wanted to create a separate nation called the Confederate States of America. The North, led by Abraham Lincoln, refused to let the southern states leave without a fight. The result was a civil war. If you study the Civil War you will discover what an important period of history it was. You will undoubtedly find that it was a fierce war in which families were torn apart, brothers fought each other, and the entire North American continent was in turmoil. You will also find fascinating characters and interesting stories of bravery, strategy, and survival. Out of the American Civil War arose the unified country that came to be called a superpower: the *United* States of America.

II. IDENTIFYING TOPICS (point III of the contract)

Use encyclopedias to identify at least ten topics that you could study about the American Civil War. Choose *one* of these topics for your project. Here are some key terms that you can look up:

A. American Civil War (or United States Civil War)

B. Abraham Lincoln

C. Jefferson Davis

D. Robert E. Lee

E. Ulysses S. Grant

F. Emancipation Proclamation

G. Slavery

H. Republicans

I. The Thirteenth and Fourteenth Amendments to the Constitution

J. The Mason-Dixon line

K. The "Missouri Compromise"

III. FINDING SOURCES (point V of the contract)

Find five sources of information about the topic. In addition to encyclopedias, there are many library books, biographies, magazine articles, filmstrips, textbooks, and other materials available about the American Civil War. You should have no difficulty locating enough sources of information to do this project.

IV. GENERAL REQUIREMENTS

A. Design a presentation that explains what you have learned.

B. You will be required to present your project to the teacher or to your class, and perhaps to other audiences.

V. PROJECT IDEAS

A. Choose an important battle and describe it.

    1. Who were the generals?

    2. Where did it occur? (Show it on a map!)

    3. Describe each army and the moves it made.

    4. Who won?

    5. What did the winner gain?

B. Make a time line of events that led up to and continued through the war.

C. Make a mobile that shows people who were involved in the American Civil War.

D. Write a report about brothers fighting brothers, fathers fighting sons, and families torn apart by the Civil War.

E. Build a diorama with cardboard cutouts showing an important event, like the Gettysburg Address.

VI. DUE DATES

A. Mid-Project Report: _____

B. Final Project: _____

AMERICAN PRESIDENTS
Student Assignment Sheet

© 1987 by The Center for Applied Research in Education, Inc.

I. INTRODUCTION

The president of the United States of America is one of the most powerful people in the world. He gets his power from the citizens who vote for him and from the Constitution, which spells out his rights and responsibilities as the representative of the people. Every president has faced trials and tribulations, victories and accomplishments. Some presidents are more obscure than others because they happened to preside over peaceful, uneventful times, or because they were not as flamboyant or outgoing as others. Have you heard of Chester Arthur, James Garfield, Warren Harding, Gerald Ford, or Calvin Coolidge? These men were all leaders of the United States—presidents. Each is a fascinating story, even though not as well known as Washington's, Lincoln's, Roosevelt's, Kennedy's, or Reagan's.

You should keep in mind that the president of the United States has not always been one of the most powerful people in the world. George Washington was leader of little more than the eastern seacoast, and was not considered an important figure in world affairs. Presidents through the entire nineteenth century were powerful inside the United States and with neighboring countries, but they had little influence with the kings, queens, and emperors who ruled the rest of the world. It wasn't until the First World War that the United States emerged as a powerful force that European and Asian leaders had to reckon with. And the title "most powerful man" was not applied to the president until the conclusion of World War II, after the defeat of Adolf Hitler and the explosion of the first atomic bomb over Japan. American presidents are some of the most interesting subjects available for research topics. No matter which one you choose, you will enjoy learning about a person who directly shaped a slice of American history.

II. IDENTIFYING TOPICS (point III of the contract)

Identify ten presidents that you would like to study and then choose *one* of these men for your project. Don't limit yourself to the most famous or familiar presidents; do some preliminary research and find out which ones made significant accomplishments or lived during a time that interests you. Also, don't preselect a president and then just list nine others. Keep your mind open until you have found information about all ten, then select the one that seems most interesting to you.

III. FINDING SOURCES (point V of the contract)

Find five sources of information about the president you have chosen. In addition to encyclopedias, look in library books, biographies, history books, magazine articles, and other materials that are available. You should have no difficulty locating enough sources of information to do this project.

IV. GENERAL REQUIREMENTS
   A. Design a presentation that explains what you have learned.
   B. You will be required to present your project to the teacher or to your class, and perhaps to other audiences.

V. PROJECT IDEAS
   A. Write a biography
      1. Date of birth and death
      2. The story of how he got elected
      3. Three or four major accomplishments while in office
      4. Early history
         a. Hometown
         b. Childhood
         c. Education
         d. Early jobs and political offices
         e. Family
      5. Whatever other information you wish to include
   B. Make a time line that shows events in the person's life or presidency.
   C. Make a mobile that shows important facts, dates, and accomplishments.
   D. Make a mural about the president's life, or his presidency: a visual biography.
   E. Build a diorama with cardboard cutouts showing an important event from the presidency of the person you have chosen.

VI. DUE DATES
   A. Mid-Project Report: _____

   B. Final Project: _____

Name _____ Date _____

THE AMERICAN REVOLUTION
Student Assignment Sheet

In CONGRESS, July 4, 1776

The unanimous Declaration of the thirteen united States of America,

When in the course of human events it becomes necessary for one people to dissolve the political bands which have connected them with another, and to assume among the powers of the earth...

I. INTRODUCTION

A "revolution" is a time when people revolt, or turn against their government. It is a time when the government has to fight against its own people to keep power and stay in control. A successful revolution brings about a change in the type of government a country has, and allows a new group of people to come to power.

The American Revolution began in 1776. The American people (not all, but many) were tired of British rule and wanted to establish a government of their own. Since the king of England (George III) refused to let America be an independent nation, there was a fight between his army and the colonists. This war was really a battle over who would rule in the 13 colonies. The war was won by the colonists and the United States of America was born. If you study the American Revolution you will learn about the birth of the most prosperous, powerful nation on earth. It is a fascinating story that you are sure to enjoy.

II. IDENTIFYING TOPICS (point III of the contract)

Use encyclopedias to identify at least ten topics that you could study about the American Revolution. Choose *one* of these topics for your project. Here are some key terms that you can look up:

A. American Revolution
B. "Intolerable Acts"
C. Benjamin Franklin
D. George Washington
E. Thomas Jefferson
F. "Common Sense"
G. Thirteen Colonies
H. Continental Congress
I. Declaration of Independence
J. Constitution
K. Minutemen
L. Boston Tea Party
M. Stamp Act

III. FINDING SOURCES (point V of the contract)

Find five sources of information about the topic. In addition to encyclopedias, there are many library books, biographies, magazine articles, filmstrips, textbooks, and other materials available about the American Revolution. You should have no difficulty locating enough sources of information to do this project.

IV. GENERAL REQUIREMENTS
   A. Design a presentation that explains what you have learned.
   B. You will be required to present your project to the teacher or to your class, and perhaps to other audiences.

V. PROJECT IDEAS
   A. Choose an important battle and describe it.
   1. Who were the generals?
   2. Where did it occur? (Show it on a map!)
   3. Describe each army and the moves it made.
   4. Who won?
   5. What did the winner gain?
   B. Make a time line of events that led up to and continued through the war.
   C. Make a mobile that shows people who were involved in the American Revolution.
   D. Write a report about Americans who did *not* want to revolt against the king of England.
   E. Build a diorama with cardboard cutouts showing an important event, like the Boston Tea Party.

VI. DUE DATES
   A. Mid-Project Report: _____

   B. Final Project: _____

ANCIENT CULTURES AND CIVILIZATIONS
Student Assignment Sheet

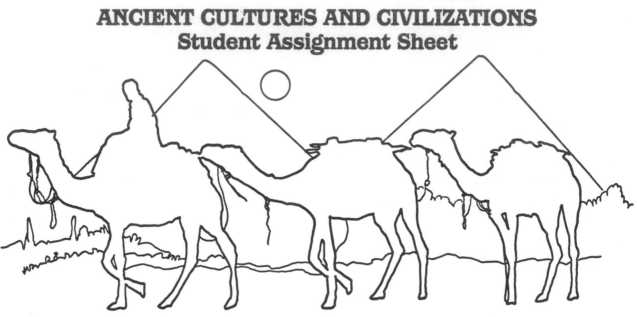

I. INTRODUCTION

Thousands of years ago human minds were at work, just as today, trying to figure out how to live and prosper on planet earth. Great civilizations rose and fell as kings and would-be kings faced their armies against one another and contested for power. Scientists studied nature, musicians played music, philosophers argued ideas, parents raised children, merchants traded goods, generals trained soldiers, farmers produced food: life went on in many predictable ways. And yet, ancient cultures were entirely different from the modern world in many ways, from religion to law. The similarities and differences between "us" and "them" are what make the study of ancient cultures and civilizations so interesting. We are, after all, direct descendants of the people who lived in the world two or three or four thousand years ago. They determined to some degree what we have become, and if we study them we are, in effect, studying ourselves in our infancy.

II. IDENTIFYING TOPICS (point III of the contract)

A. Before choosing a specific topic, decide upon an ancient civilization to study. On the contract (if you are using one for this project) write "Ancient Cultures and Civilizations" on the line marked "Project Title" under point II. On the next line, marked "Subtitle," record the civilization you have chosen to study. You may choose from the following list, or find one of your own:

1. Egypt
2. Mesopotamia
3. Sumer
4. Greece
5. Persia

6. Phoenicia
7. Babylonia
8. Rome
9. Assyria
10. The Han dynasty (China)

B. Use encyclopedias to identify at least ten topics that you could study about the civilization you have chosen. Choose *one* of these topics for your project. Here are some ideas of things you can look up:

1. Kings, emperors, or rulers
2. Religions
3. Wars and battles
4. Festivals and ceremonies
5. Famous people
6. Trade, commerce, and transportation

7. Agriculture and food supplies
8. Enemies and bordering kingdoms
9. Daily life
10. Arts, crafts, writings, and architecture
11. Medicine

III. FINDING SOURCES (point V of the contract)

Find five sources of information about the topic. In addition to encyclopedias, there are many library books, biographies, magazine articles, filmstrips, textbooks, and other materials available about ancient cultures and civilizations. You should have no difficulty locating enough sources of information to do this project if you are careful about topic selection.

IV. GENERAL REQUIREMENTS

A. Design a presentation that explains what you have learned.

B. You will be required to present your project to the teacher or to your class, and perhaps to other audiences.

V. PROJECT IDEAS

A. Choose an important war and describe who was in it, who won it, and what the results were. Use maps to show where the conflict occurred.

B. Make a time line that shows what civilizations existed *before* the one you have chosen, and what came after. Use the time line to point out important events during the time that your civilization was in existence.

C. Make a mobile that shows people and events from the civilization you have chosen to study.

D. Make a mural that shows lifestyles or events from your civilization.

E. Build a diorama with cardboard cutouts that shows the daily life of the people, such as: a religious ceremony, preparing food, meeting on the battlefield, trading goods, traveling, and so forth.

VI. DUE DATES

A. Mid-Project Report: _____

B. Final Project: _____

BIRTH OF A SUPERPOWER: THE RUSSIAN REVOLUTION
Student Assignment Sheet

I. INTRODUCTION

There are many countries in the world today, but there are only two nations that are referred to as "superpowers." One of these superpowers is very familiar to you because you are a citizen, and it is your country. The United States is, indeed, a superpower. Because of its size, its wealth, its influence, and most importantly, its military and nuclear arsenal, America ranks as the most powerful country in the world. You have known about the United States and its people and history since the day you were born—but what do you know about the other superpower? The Union of Soviet Socialist Republics (U.S.S.R. or Soviet Union), with a nuclear arsenal roughly equal to that of America's, is continually in the news and on the minds of Americans; yet we know very little about it. The purpose of this project is to introduce you to the period of history that produced the U.S.S.R.: The Russian Revolution.

"Russia" was the name of a country before the Russian revolution occurred; after the revolution, this country became the most powerful and populous state in the Soviet Union. Before 1917 Russia was ruled by an emperor who was called a tsar (zär), which is sometimes spelled czar, csar, and tzar. Ivan the Terrible was the first tsar, who ruled from 1533 to 1584. The last tsar was Nicholas II, who ruled from 1894 to 1917. In 1917 the Russian Revolution ended Nicholas's reign, and Russia became a state in the Soviet Union. By studying the Russian Revolution you will learn about the people who brought the revolution about and you will begin to understand the events that gave birth to communism in the world. This is an important and worthwhile project to work on, and if you are careful about choosing a topic, it is a project you will enjoy doing.

II. IDENTIFYING TOPICS (point III of the contract)

Use encyclopedias to identify at least ten topics that you could study about the Russian Revolution. Choose *one* of these topics for your project. Here are some key terms that you can look up:

A. Communism
B. Russian Revolution
C. Bolsheviks
D. V.I. Lenin
E. Leon Trotsky
F. Joseph Stalin
G. World War I
H. Provisional Government
I. Mensheviks
J. Treaty of Brest-Litovsk
K. Nicholas II

III. FINDING SOURCES (point V of the course)

Find five sources of information about the topic. In addition to encyclopedias, there are many library books, biographies, history books, textbooks, filmstrips, and other materials available about the Russian Revolution. You should have no problem locating enough sources of information to do this project.

IV. GENERAL REQUIREMENTS

A. Design a presentation that explains what you have learned.

B. You will be required to present your project to the teacher or to your class, and perhaps to other audiences.

V. PROJECT IDEAS

A. Choose a person who played an important role in the Russian Revolution and write his or her biography.

B. Make a time line of events that led up to and continued through the revolution. You can continue your time line through World War II if you wish.

C. Make a mobile that shows events in a person's life, or facts about the topic you have chosen to study.

D. Make a mural that shows the sequence of events that led to the downfall of Nicholas II.

E. Build a diorama with cardboard cutouts showing an important event from the Russian Revolution, like the capture of the tsar's train or the signing of the Treaty of Brest-Litovsk.

VI. DUE DATES

A. Mid-Project Report: _____

B. Final Project: _____

BLACK HISTORY
Student Assignment Sheet

I. INTRODUCTION

Black people have lived in America since the early 1600s. They have made major contributions to American culture in all areas, including education, science, medicine, law, music, technology, politics, philosophy, religion, civil rights, athletics, entertainment, labor, and literature. Blacks have had to combat racism and prejudice in their struggle to achieve the American dream. For the first 250 years of their presence in North America most blacks had to endure the humiliation and suffering of slavery. The Emancipation Proclamation (signed by Abraham Lincoln in 1863) and the Thirteenth Amendment to the Constitution (passed in 1865) abolished slavery in the United States. Since then, blacks have worked hard to gain the rights that citizenship in America guarantees. It has been a difficult road, with many peaks and valleys. The story of black people in America is a fascinating one, filled with tragedy and triumph, perseverance and accomplishment. Black history is an important field of study, one that holds many keys to understanding the history of the United States of America. Your research will give you valuable insights into our modern society and current black issues.

II. IDENTIFYING TOPICS (point III of the contract)

Use encyclopedias to identify at least ten topics that you could study about black history. Choose *one* of these topics for your project. Here are some key terms that you can look up:

A. Emancipation Proclamation
B. Thirteenth Amendment to the U.S. Constitution
C. Dred Scott
D. Dr. Martin Luther King, Jr.
E. Underground railroad
F. The Rev. Jesse Jackson
G. Civil rights
H. Rosa Parks
I. NAACP
J. Voting Rights Act

III. FINDING SOURCES (point V of the contract)

Find five sources of information about the topic. In addition to encyclopedias, there are many library sources, biographies, magazine articles, filmstrips, textbooks, and other materials available about black history. You should have no difficulty locating enough information to do this project. Don't overlook an obvious resource: people who can provide personal experiences and insights that relate to your research topic.

IV. GENERAL REQUIREMENTS

A. Design a presentation that explains what you have learned.

B. You will be required to present your project to the teacher or to your class, and perhaps to other audiences.

V. PROJECT IDEAS

A. Choose a person and conduct an in-depth study of him or her.

    1. Write a biography.

    2. Write a report that explains how this person affected history.

    3. Design a poster that shows major events from this person's life.

B. Make a time line of events that have had an influence on the lives of black people, and of the accomplishments of black people since the seventeenth century.

C. Make a mobile showing various key people in black history and explaining what they did in their lives.

D. Make a mural that shows a certain portion of the black experience in America, such as famous musicians or contributions to science.

E. Build a diorama with cardboard cutouts showing an important event, like Dr. Martin Luther King, Jr., delivering his famous "I Have a Dream" speech.

VI. DUE DATES

A. Mid-Project Report: _____

B. Final Project: _____

Name _____ Date _____

CAREER EXPLORATION
Student Assignment Sheet

SPECIAL NOTE: You will need a tape recorder for this project.

I. INTRODUCTION

You have probably been asked many times, "What do you want to be when you grow up?" Did you have an answer, or were you unsure of what career you would choose? If you know "what you want to be," how did you make that decision? Many times people choose to go into occupations without knowing what the job involves. They often make a career decision based on a glamorous image they picked up from television or some other media. If you are interested in a particular area of work it is a good idea to talk with someone who chose it as a career. It is worthwhile to find out what experienced people have to say about a job. Through interviews you can learn many important details that may not be available in books or pamphlets. When it comes time for you to make a decision about your future, you will want to choose a career that is right for *you,* one that makes use of your strengths and abilities. This project lets you explore several different careers in which you might be interested. You must be willing to talk to people to become involved in this project because it requires you to contact and interview adults in various occupations. As you talk with each person, pay close attention to what he or she says. Ask yourself if this is something you could be happy doing and whether it fits your personality and life goals.

II. IDENTIFYING TOPICS (point III of the contract)

Write ten questions that you want to ask during each interview. Some examples are given in Section IV of this handout but you are expected to think of some on your own. No doubt you have questions about each job area that you would like answered, and these should be written so that they require more than a "yes" or "no" answer. It might be helpful to watch several news shows to find out how questions are phrased and to study interviewing techniques used by professionals. The idea is to get people to talk about their jobs.

NOTE: Point IV of the "Individualized Project Contract" is not to be used with this project. You may leave it blank.

III. FINDING SOURCES (point V of the contract)

List the names and occupations of five people you could call if you are given approval for this project. Even though you will actually interview only three, it is wise to have alternates ready in case your first choice can't meet with you. You will interview people from three *different* occupations for this project. If you want to concentrate on one occupation you must get special permission.

IV. GENERAL REQUIREMENTS

A. Select three careers that you want to study. You may want to select from among these examples:

1. Store owner (often called a "merchant")
2. Minister (or priest or rabbi)
3. Doctor
4. Dentist
5. Lawyer
6. School teacher
7. School principal
8. City worker
9. Social worker
10. Factory worker
11. Government worker
12. Politician
13. Nurse or medical technician
14. Secretary
15. Mechanic
16. Policeman or policewoman
17. Banker
18. Professional athlete

B. Contact three people (one from each career), and ask them for interviews. They can be people you know, but they don't have to be. You will find all kinds of professional people who are willing to sit down with you and talk about careers. Each interview will be conducted with a tape recorder. Here are a few sample questions:

1. Why or how did you become interested in your job?
2. What kinds of experience and education does your job require?
3. What kinds of things do you do in your job?
4. Are there any things a person my age can do to get ready to do a job like yours?
5. What kinds of classes should a high school student who is interested in your occupation take?
6. What other kinds of occupations might your job lead toward?
7. Would you advise a young person to try to get into your occupation area?
8. Do you think there will be new occupational opportunities in the future?
9. Is your job different than you expected it to be before you took it? How?

C. After you have interviewed three people and recorded the interviews on tape, write a paper for each of the three occupations. If you want, you can "transcribe" the tapes for your report. This means that you write down, word-for-word, what was said on the tape:

Question: Why did you become interested in your job?
Answer: Because I...
Question: What kinds of things do you do in your job?
Answer: I do a lot of different things,...

V. PROJECT IDEAS

A. If someone you want to interview is very busy and difficult to contact by phone you could write a one-page letter explaining your project and ask for an appointment. Enclose a self-addressed postcard with a place for the person to check "yes" or "no" to your request and leave a space for the person to write you a note about a convenient meeting time. Give your phone number in the letter so you can be contacted about the interview. Remember: what you say in your letter or on the phone should be thought through so that the person you are contacting knows you are serious about the interview. Have the things you want to say on the phone written down so you don't forget important details. This will give the person you are going to meet a good impression of you and a positive attitude about your project.

B. If you know the person you are going to interview quite well, and if you have a camera, you may want to take several pictures to help illustrate the report. Be sure to discuss this with the person before the meeting.

C. There is career information available in libraries, school counseling centers, and college campuses that you may want to include with your reports. If it is current information it is worth checking into.

D. In addition to the report, you can visually present the information you've gathered on a poster, mural, or mobile.

VI. DUE DATES

A. Mid-Project Report: _____

B. Final Project: _____

VII. WRITTEN PERMISSION

I am aware that my son/daughter _____
(Student's name)
wants to interview three adults about their occupations. I will be responsible for knowing who these people are and when and where my child will meet with them. I also understand I may have to provide transportation for these interviews.

_____
(Parent signature)

Parent, please check one:

_____ Yes, if necessary, I can provide a tape recorder and a tape for this project.

_____ I do not have access to a tape recorder but I am willing to provide a tape.

_____ I cannot provide a tape recorder or a tape.

CURRENT EVENTS BULLETIN BOARD
Student Assignment Sheet

I. INTRODUCTION

The world seems to be a much smaller place than it used to be. In Thomas Jefferson's day it took six weeks for news in Europe to reach America. Writing a letter and sending it by boat was the fastest way news could travel across the Atlantic. Now, with the technology of communication satellites, television pictures as well as words can be beamed around the world in seconds. Each day through the news media we can learn what has happened on every continent in the last 24 hours.

Investors, politicians, business people, doctors, weather forecasters, scientists, and military officials all depend on instant communication to do their jobs. Many times decisions about our own personal lives depend on what we hear in the news. Would you continue with your plans to go camping if tornadoes were being predicted for your area? If your family were getting ready to buy a house and you read that interest rates would start going up in six months, wouldn't it make sense to buy a home as soon as possible in order to save money? And isn't it important for us to be informed about world events in general?

This project is designed to help you learn about what is going on in the world. Some of the news you read may not seem important but other news will interest you very much. You will keep track of current events and make a bulletin board display of specific topics you choose to study. Your bulletin board will consist of a world map and brief explanations of important events that are currently happening. Since so much news is reported every week it will be a challenge for you to select just two current events each day to include on your display.

II. IDENTIFYING TOPICS (point III of the contract)

Before you will be allowed to work on this project, you must identify ten current events/topics that you would be interested in studying. These topics may be very different from each other. For example: wars, medicine, weather, science, politics, celebrations, tragedies, personalities, government, and so forth. From this list of ten topics, choose at least two that you would most like to report about. NOTE: If you are filling out an "Individualized Study Contract" for this project you will list *at least two topics* under point IV of the contract as ones you want to study. Do not list more than five.

III. FINDING SOURCES (point V of the contract)

Find five sources of information which you can use to learn about your topics. These can include newspapers, weekly news magazines, television news reports, and special television programs. Be specific and list the name of each source you plan to use.

IV. GENERAL REQUIREMENTS

A. You will be given bulletin board space and a map of the world. The map will be placed in the middle of the bulletin board.

B. You will write daily about *two* current events on 5-by-8-inch notecards (one event per card) and tack the cards around the map on the bulletin board. These current events will relate to one of the topics you chose to focus on for this project. Every event should be dated. Make a bibliography that tells where your facts came from. Your information *must* be accurate.

C. From each card you will run a piece of colored string to the place in the world where the event happened, and pin the string to the map. For example, if you write about a drought in Everglades National Park, you will pin a colored string to the information card and run it to the southern tip of Florida on the world map.

D. You will add two more cards each day for three weeks. Remember, put as much quality as you possibly can into this project. Don't be satisfied with anything but your best work. Your current events cards need not be long, but they should be informative and attractive.

E. The current events topics can be things that happened in the recent past. None of the events should be more than one year old. Newspapers and magazines will be important sources of information, as will TV news and discussions with your family.

F. The main purpose of the project is to teach other people about what is currently happening in the world, so make your notecards *informative, accurate,* and *easy to understand.*

V. PROJECT IDEAS

A. If you have access to a computer you may want to use it to write about each of your current events and tack up the printouts instead of handwritten notecards. Some computers allow you to choose boldface type or special letter styles which would add interest to your bulletin board.

B. If you are studying three different areas of current events you could use three different colors of fine-line markers to write out your notecards. For example, cards written in blue could all be about energy, cards written in red could be about environmental pollution, and cards written in green could be about government leaders. Color can be used very effectively in other ways to make your display more attractive.

C. Don't overlook the possibility of using pictures out of newspapers and magazines or your own drawings to help illustrate your written information. The focus of the bulletin board, however, is the world map and you should do whatever is necessary so that it shows clearly where the events on the notecards happened.

VI. DUE DATES

A. Mid-Project Report: _____

B. Final Project: _____

Name _____ Date _____

CURRENT NEWS SCRAPBOOK
Student Assignment Sheet

I. INTRODUCTION

For this project you will make a scrapbook of current events for one month. When it is completed it will become a slice of history that identifies many news topics that happened during four weeks of your life. It is surprising how interesting a book like this will be after a few years when you take it off the shelf and look at it again. Headlines that were once current will have faded into the past, but you will be able to remember them personally since you wrote about them the day they happened.

Making a current events scrapbook is fun if you put your own creativity into it. Select news stories that interest you or that you think will become important points in history. Some general news categories that you may wish to investigate are

A. Scientific discoveries, inventions, and theories
B. Unusual or severe weather
C. Wars, riots, demonstrations, acts of terrorism
D. Peace talks and the latest weapon development
E. World leaders and their policies
F. Social issues
G. Significant court cases or decisions
H. Popular fads and fashions
I. Medical advancements or breakthroughs
J. Special events
K. Special people

You should also design an attractive or eye-catching cover for the book, put glue carefully on the back of clipped articles so that it doesn't cause pages to stick together, use your best handwriting and, basically, put your best effort into your work so that it's worth doing.

This project will make you more aware of the fact that an entire world full of people is thinking, discovering, reacting, laughing, suffering, and changing while you grow up in your own little neighborhood. It is a good investment to teach yourself about the world you live in and to evaluate what you learn. You will then be better able to make decisions about your life, based on reality.

II. IDENTIFYING TOPICS (point III of the contract)

Before you begin this project, look through newspapers or news magazines and identify ten important current events that interest you. This means *specific* topics like, "The Present War in Central America," "New Information About a Healthy Diet," or "Effects of Drought in Africa." In other words, someone reading this list should be able to tell specifically what kinds of events are in the news. This preliminary work will help you decide which topic you would like to emphasize most in the scrapbook.

NOTE: If you are filling out an "Individualized Study Contract" for this project, write the news topic you want to emphasize *most* under point IV of the contract. You are not limited to articles about this topic, however. You may include many other types of news stories in your project.

III. FINDING SOURCES (point V of the contract)

List five sources that you know you can use for your scrapbook. Remember, you will clip articles from newspapers and magazines so be sure this is okay with other family members who want to read them. You may also use television news shows as sources, and take information in the form of notes that can be rewritten in your own words and entered into the book.

IV. GENERAL REQUIREMENTS

A. Choose *at least* two news stories each day and put these into the scrapbook in chronological order. If you are writing a news entry from a television report be sure to give it a headline just as if it were being read from a newspaper.

B. Put the *date* and *name* of the source under *each* entry. If it is based on an evening news program put the name of the program under your written entry. You may also want to include the name of the reporter.

C. Make entries in your scrapbook for five days of each week for one month (20 days total). This means you will have at least 40 articles in your finished project.

D. Number the pages in your book.

E. Make an index for the scrapbook before handing it in. This index should include your main current events in alphabetical order. Under each current event write the headlines from your book and the pages they are found on. For example:

Effects of Drought in Africa (Current event, listed in alphabetical order)

- Starvation Spreading in Ethiopia, pg. 2 (headline)
- Former Forest Land Now Desert, pg. 4 (headline)
- Economy Devastated by Drought, pg. 7 (headline)
- Children Main Victims of Drought, pg. 11 (headline)

F. Think of a name or title for your scrapbook.

V. PROJECT IDEAS

A. If you have a video recorder you could record news programs and play them back again later to be sure you got the information you need to write reports.

B. You may want to purchase a commercially made scrapbook that has a hard cover and oversized, blank pages on which you can carefully glue the articles. Or, you can easily construct your own scrapbook using drawing paper. A very attractive cover can be made by putting cloth over thick cardboard or by cutting holes for metal rings in two pieces of masonite or thin plywood. A strong cover will keep your scrapbook looking good for many years.

C. A good way to decide which articles to clip is to go through a paper or magazine and put a small check mark next to each headline that interests you. Then go back and choose the best ones for your scrapbook.

VI. DUE DATES

A. Mid-Project Report: _____

B. Final Project: _____

© 1987 by The Center for Applied Research in Education, Inc.

Name _____ Date _____

ECONOMICS: PRICES NOW AND THEN
Student Assignment Sheet

I. INTRODUCTION

Economics is the study of the production, distribution, sale, and use of goods and products. It is also the study of money and how money is used to buy goods, products, and services. There is a reason why you have to pay a certain amount for a product like a bicycle. The costs of materials, manufacturing, labor, shipping, and displaying a bicycle for sale must all be added into the final price tag, plus whatever profit the manufacturer wants, plus a profit for the store that sells it. If any of these costs increase, the price of the bicycle will increase too. If the price of the bicycle rises too much, people won't buy it and the manufacturer and the store owner will have to figure out ways to cut their costs. If this is impossible, they must stop making and selling the bicycle.

Over the years since the end of World War II (1945) prices for almost everything have generally gone up. Why haven't people stopped buying things? Because over this same period of time wages and salaries have also increased. This project focuses on the price differences between now and the past, going back to the Great Depression of the 1930s. You will be amazed at how little some things cost in the 1930s, 1940s, 1950s, and 1960s. A gallon of gasoline, for example, cost about 30 cents before 1970. "Economics: Prices Now and Then" gives you an opportunity to learn about the value of money and American economics. If you want to know more about money and how it works, you will enjoy this project.

II. IDENTIFYING TOPICS (point III of the contract)

A. This project is designed to let you compare prices and other economic facts and figures from the past with those of today. Before choosing a specific topic, decide upon a five-year period from American history that you want to compare with the present. On the contract (if you are using one for this project) write "Economics: Prices Now and Then" on the line marked "Project Title" under point II. On the next line, marked "Subtitle," record the five-year period you have chosen:

1. 1930–35
2. 1935–40
3. 1940–45
4. 1945–50
5. 1950–55
6. 1955–60
7. 1960–65
8. 1965–70
9. 1970–75
10. 1975–80
11. 1980–85

The subtitle should read like this: "Comparison Between 1945–50 and the Present."

135

B. List ten topics that you could study to make comparisons between the past and the present. Choose at least *one* of these topics for your project but you may include more if you wish. Here are some ideas of things you can look up:

1. Prices and costs of transportation (automobiles, airline, train, and bus tickets)
2. Prices and costs of food
3. Prices and costs of housing
4. Prices and costs of household goods, appliances, luxury items, and clothing
5. Average income for various groups of Americans:

   a. Blacks
   b. Whites
   c. Blue-collar workers (union/nonunion)
   d. White-collar workers
   e. Doctors, lawyers, engineers, teachers, scientists, and other professions

   f. College-educated
   g. Professional athletes
   h. Entertainers
   i. Soldiers
   j. Etc.

6. Gross National Product
7. Taxes
8. Federal budget
9. Military spending
10. Welfare, social security, medicare, other social programs

III. FINDING SOURCES (point V of the contract)

Find five sources of information about your topic or topics. Encyclopedias will be useful, but your most valuable source will be microfilm copies of newspapers and magazines from the years you have chosen to study and actual newspapers and magazines from today. In addition to these materials, you will also find information in almanacs, statistics books, census data, government budget figures and pamphlets produced by various departments of federal and state governments. Finally, there are library books, history books, textbooks, and other materials available about economics that you can use.

IV. GENERAL REQUIREMENTS

A. Design a presentation that explains what you have learned.
B. You will be required to present your project to the teacher or to your class, and perhaps to other audiences.

V. PROJECT IDEAS

A. Make a graph that shows the difference between prices during your five-year period of history and those of today.
B. Make a poster that explains such terms as "GNP," "balance of trade," "per capita income," and "poverty level," and show comparisons between today and your five-year historical period.
C. Make a mobile that shows prices now and prices during your five-year period. Each cutout in the mobile can represent a certain item or commodity; one side would show how much the item costs today and the other side would show how much the same item cost in the past.
D. Make a mural that shows the differences in costs of things now and in the past, such as military spending, automobiles, or food.
E. Make a collage that shows: a wide variety of items and their costs; economic terms and their definitions; or statistics and their meanings. Each example on your collage should be accompanied by "now" and "then" information.

VI. DUE DATES

A. Mid-Project Report: _____

B. Final Project: _____

THE GREAT DEPRESSION
Student Assignment Sheet

THE GREAT CRASH——

OCTOBER, 1929						
SUNDAY	MONDAY	TUESDAY	WEDNESDAY	THURSDAY	FRIDAY	SATURDAY
		1	2	3	4	5
6	7	8	9	10	11	12
13	14	15	16	17	18	19
20	21	22	23	24 BLACK THURSDAY	25	26
27	28	29	30	31		

I. INTRODUCTION

A "depression" is a time when unemployment is very high. It is a period of low economic activity during which people don't have money to invest or spend. A depression causes a decrease in manufacturing and money supplies, which leads to a loss of jobs.

The entire world went through a depression in the 1930s. This was the "Great Depression." During this time many people lost businesses, homes, farms, and fortunes. It was a time of tragedy for millions, in the United States and elsewhere. You can find people who still remember the Great Depression, and their memories are valuable sources of information. If you study the Great Depression you will learn about one of the most trying times in American history. You will find that this is an extraordinary story of people overcoming hard times. You will also find that the Great Depression produced a man in Europe named Adolf Hitler and planted the seeds for World War II.

II. IDENTIFYING TOPICS (point III of the contract)

Use encyclopedias to identify at least ten topics that you could study about the Great Depression. Your project will focus on one or more of the topics you list; record the topic you are *most* interested in on the contract (point IV). Here are some key terms that you can look up:

A. Great Depression
B. Herbert Hoover
C. Franklin Roosevelt
D. New Deal
E. Dust Bowl
F. Black Thursday

III. FINDING SOURCES (point V of the contract)

Find five sources of information about the topic. You can include, as sources, people who lived through the Great Depression. There is also a tremendous number of books, magazine articles, filmstrips, textbooks, and other materials about the Great Depression available in the library. You should not have difficulty locating enough sources of information to do this project.

IV. GENERAL REQUIREMENTS
   A. Design a presentation that explains what you have learned.
   B. You will be required to present your project to the teacher or to your class, and perhaps to other audiences.

V. PROJECT IDEA: Use a tape recorder to interview people who lived during the depression.
   A. Ideal subjects would be grandparents, great-grandparents, and great-aunts and uncles.
   B. Ask questions that will help you understand the depression better. Each question should relate to one or more of the ten topics you listed and focus primarily on the topic you chose to research. Here are some examples of interview questions:
   1. How was life during the 1920s; what were the "roarin' twenties"? How did things change in 1929?
   2. Did the depression strike suddenly, or did it creep up slowly? How did it affect banks? How did the bank situation affect people and businesses?
   3. Did the depression affect your life greatly? How?
   4. What kinds of jobs were available? How did your father earn a living?
   5. What caused the depression? What was the "New Deal"?
   6. Do you know what a a "Hooverville" was? Did you ever see one?
   7. How did life differ between the city and the country?
   8. How did the United States get out of the depression?
   9. Are we in danger of going into another depression?

   C. Combine your interview information with your other research material to produce a final presentation.

VI. DUE DATES
   A. Mid-Project Report: _____

   B. Final Project: _____

HISTORIC FIGURES
Student Assignment Sheet

I. INTRODUCTION

Throughout the ages history has been changed or directed by individuals who had the power, authority, intelligence, or special opportunity to affect the destiny of the human race. Alexander the Great conquered the entire world as he knew it, from Greece to India. When he was a young man his father (Phillip of Macedon) died, leaving him an army that was trained in new kinds of warfare and was poised for battle. Alexander, using power, authority, intelligence, *and* opportunity, left his name on history forever.

The list of historic figures is almost endless: world leaders, religious leaders, scientists, inventors, military leaders, royalty, spies, heroes, philosophers, politicians, entertainers, explorers, and many others. It is, after all, *people* who create history. History is merely the story of people living their lives and leaving their marks on the world. As you study the life of a famous person you will make an amazing discovery: there are people who have lived far more interesting lives than any fictional charcter ever invented. Can you imagine sailing off into an ocean that many people were certain ended in a huge waterfall protected by sea monsters? That's what Christopher Columbus did! What would it be like to invent something that changed the whole world forever, as Thomas Edison did with the lightbulb and Wilbur and Orville Wright did with the airplane? Study Mozart or Bach or Beethoven to find out more about the human beings who wrote such beautiful music that people still love it hundreds of years later. The number of exciting people to study is astronomical and the historic events you can explore are without limit. Choose carefully, and you will have a project that really captures your attention and interest.

II. IDENTIFYING TOPICS (point III of the contract)

Identify ten people that you would like to study. These people cannot be living today; special permission is required to study a living person. Spend some time looking through encyclopedias and history books to find interesting people that you may not have heard of but who have played an important role in history.

Choose *one* of these people for your project. If you already know whom you are going to study, you still must list nine other people, so make it worthwhile: find people who worked with, or were associated with, the person you have chosen. This will help in later research. Here are some terms that you can look up to help find the names of historic figures:

A. Inventors
B. Explorers
C. Presidents
D. The name of any country: France, Germany, Greece, Mexico, China, India, Syria, Egypt, and so forth
E. Royalty
F. Industrialists
G. Military history; the name of any war
H. Olympics
I. The name of any state in America
J. Music, dance, art, and so forth

III. FINDING SOURCES (point V of the contract)

Find five sources of information about the person you have chosen. In addition to encyclopedias, you can look in library books, biographies, history books, magazine articles, and other materials that are available to you. Be careful in your topic selection: be sure there is enough information available before you definitely decide upon a person to study.

IV. GENERAL REQUIREMENTS

A. Design a presentation that explains what you have learned.
B. You will be required to present your project to the teacher or to your class, and perhaps to other audiences.

V. PROJECT IDEAS

A. Write a biography.
   1. Date of birth and death
   2. Three or four major accomplishments
   3. Hometown and other important places
   4. Family information
   5. Explanation of what role the person played in history
   6. Whatever other information is available

B. Make a time line that shows events in the person's life.
C. Make a mobile that shows the accomplishments of the person, and some important dates and facts
D. Make a mural about the person's life: a visual biography.
E. Build a diorama with cardboard cutouts showing an important event from the person's life.

VI. DUE DATES

A. Mid-Project Report: _____

B. Final Project: _____

© 1987 by The Center for Applied Research in Education, Inc.

Name _____ Date _____

LETTER TO THE EDITOR
Student Assignment Sheet

I. INTRODUCTION

Writing a letter to the editor of your local newspaper is a good way to voice your opinion about something. Newspapers advocate freedom of speech, and one way they make this freedom available to everyone is by publishing letters that are sent to the editor. Your letter should focus on an issue that is important to you or that you feel strongly about. If you want your ideas and opinions to be taken seriously, you must state your case completely and accurately with as few words as possible. Don't just blow off steam about something that angers you; carefully describe the situation so people can see that you have a *right* to be angry, and then explain what *you* would do to solve the problem if you had the power or authority. If you offer an opinion with your letter, support it with facts and sound reasoning. Try to avoid statements like "I think they ought to make a law that lets kids have ten months of vacation a year." Really? For whose benefit? Would this be in your best interests? How about America's? Your readers would wonder about your sincerity if you wrote such a thing to the editor. Your letter *must* be sincere.

You will write one letter for this project and you will send it to the editor of your local newspaper. Choose your subject carefully, and use your best writing skills. Don't write anything embarrassing or ridiculous: remember! Your name will be published with the letter and everyone will know who wrote it!

II. IDENTIFYING TOPICS (point III of the contract)

Identify ten issues or topics about which you could write a letter to the editor. You will choose *one* of these topics for your project. The topics you list may be local, state, national, or international issues, or they may be things that you have on your mind that you would like to express to others. There are so many different topic possibilities that it is impossible to list them all. You are encouraged to think of ten topics on your own, but here are a few suggestions that may help you get started:

A. Discipline in school
B. Excellence in education (do we have it?)
C. Child abuse
D. Goals for the future
E. Parental responsibilities
F. The role school should play in a student's life
G. Moneymaking opportunities for people under 18 years old
H. Violence on television
I. Smoking
J. Drugs and alcohol (especially mixed with driving)

III. FINDING SOURCES (point V of the contract)

The contract requires that you find five sources of information before beginning a project, but that is not necessary for writing a letter to the editor. Keep in mind, however, that any statements you make should be backed by facts. It is to your advantage to find information about the topic just to ensure the accuracy of what you say. On the contract write "Not needed for this project" on the first line under point V.

IV. GENERAL REQUIREMENTS

A. Decide upon an issue or topic to write about.
B. Write a well-composed letter to the editor, stating your opinion about the topic or issue you have chosen.
C. Your letter will be signed by you, but use your school for the return address so that your home address is not published.
D. Turn your finished letter in to the teacher before sending it. You must do this to get credit for the project.

V. DUE DATE: _____

MY HOME STATE
Student Assignment Sheet

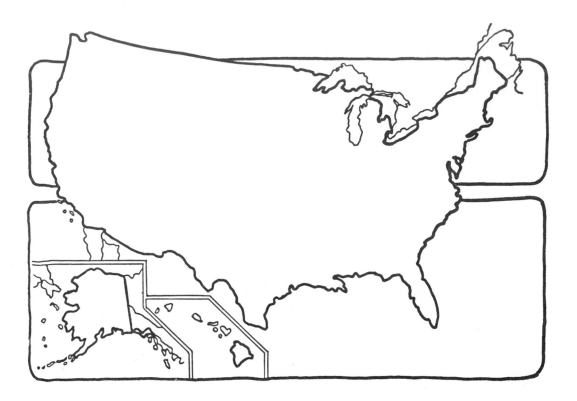

I. INTRODUCTION

America is a country composed of fifty states. The term "United States of America" refers to the fact that there are fifty parts united into a whole: a nation of small governments represented by a central government. When someone asks you where you are from, you usually respond by giving the name of your town and your home state: "I'm from Grand Rapids, Michigan." Most people identify with the state in which they were born and raised; it is not unusual to hear people call themselves "Hoosiers" or "Texans" or some other name relating to a home state.

Studying your home state is an interesting undertaking. Every state has a unique history and its own list of famous people and events. You will find that your state has places to visit, valuable resources, important industries and many other fascinating things to study. This project offers an excellent opportunity to learn about the place where you live and the people who live (or have lived) in your state. There are a lot of topics to choose from; choose carefully and you will develop a truly enjoyable project.

II. IDENTIFYING TOPICS (point III of the contract)

A. On the contract (if you are using one for this project) write "My Home State" on the line marked "Project Title" under point II. On the next line, marked "Subtitle," record what state you live in.

B. Identify at least ten topics that you could study about your home state. Your project can include one, several or all of these topics, depending upon whether you want to focus on a single topic or do a more general study about your state. The decision of how many topics you will cover is left to you, but list ten of them on the contract. Here are some areas you may want to examine:

1. Bordering states
2. Geography
3. Exploration
4. History
5. Famous people
6. Population
7. Land division
8. Governor and legislature
9. Natural resources
10. Primary industries
11. How and when your state joined the union
12. State bird, flower, song, flag, motto, nickname, and so forth
13. Tourist attractions
14. Agriculture
15. Transportation: roads, highways, rivers, railroads, airports, and so forth
16. Economy: taxes, average income, welfare, federal aid, and so forth

III. FINDING SOURCES (point V of the contract)

Find five sources of information about your topic. In addition to encyclopedias, there are many library books, textbooks, history books, magazine articles, filmstrips, and other materials available about your home state. The local library may have a special section devoted to your state, its people and history. You may also want to write letters to get information. Ask the teacher and your librarian to help locate addresses of people to whom you can send requests for information.

IV. GENERAL REQUIREMENTS

A. Design a presentation that explains what you have learned.
B. You will be required to present your project to the teacher or to your class, and perhaps to other audiences.

V. PROJECT IDEA

Make a large wall map, or a tabletop relief map, and fill it (or surround it) with information about your state:

A. Cities and towns
B. Rivers, mountains, and borders
C. Information about any or all of the areas listed for you in point II of this handout.
D. Other ideas:

1. Hang an informative mobile above or in front of your map.
2. Make a collage of information and place it next to your map.
3. Produce a poster of facts, events, and people that can be placed beside your map.

VI. DUE DATES

A. Mid-Project Report: _____

B. Final Project: _____

Name _____ Date _____

MY NEIGHBORHOOD
Student Assignment Sheet

MY SCHOOL   THE TRACKS   CRAZY BOB'S STORE   MY HOUSE

SPECIAL NOTE: You will need a camera for this project.

I. INTRODUCTION

You probably have pictures of yourself when you were younger that are fun to look at. You may also have pictures of special occasions such as parties, family get-togethers, or trips you took, that bring back memories. These photographs are a record of your own personal history, and they become more and more valuable as the years go by.

There are things in your life that you will remember and talk about when you are older but probably won't have pictures of; your favorite hang-out, the school you attend, a local store where you buy soda pop or candy, the firehouse closest to your home, a building you walk by that has character or interesting architectural design, a picture of you doing your paper route. These places and events are all part of your life and are unique to your neighborhood. This project will show and preserve in pictures important moments from your personal history. It will also teach you about the history and current events of the place where you are growing up.

For the first part of your project you will need a camera and a 12-exposure roll of color print film in order to make your visual display. You should understand that this project is not designed to teach photography and that you must know how to use a camera on your own. Before you decide to do "My Neighborhood," get permission from a parent to show that you have a camera to use and can pay for the film and processing. Using a camera to document your neighborhood is a special type of research, and you should put some thought into what you want to photograph. Examine the project ideas and plan each picture before you go out with your camera. You may not get perfect pictures but they will mean a lot to you because you planned them and took them yourself.

The second part of this project involves finding information and writing a report about your hometown. For instance, do you know what year your hometown was established? Do you know its population or what industries support the economy? You will conduct research to gather information for your report.

II. IDENTIFYING TOPICS (Parts III & IV of the contract)

Before you begin to work on this project, identify at least ten places, people, or things from your neighborhood that you want to photograph and write captions for. You will take a picture of *each* of these "topics" after they have been approved by your teacher, so be sure they are things you can photograph with your camera. A picture of a fire truck racing down the street sounds like a good idea but how long would you have to sit in front of the fire station to get that idea on film? You will list ten topics but you have 12 exposures on your film. Use the remaining two exposures in whatever way you think best.

NOTE: If you are filling out an "Individualized Study Contract" for this project, ignore point IV of the contract since *each* of your pictures is a topic that will be used.

III. FINDING SOURCES (Part V of the contract)

Find five sources of information for your written report before you begin your project. You may use local newspapers, books about your hometown, and people who have lived in the area for many years. The local library, museum, historical society, Chamber of Commerce, and other community organizations may know of other resources about your community that are available to you.

IV. GENERAL REQUIREMENTS

A. Make a visual display of your photographs, complete with captions. These captions can be more than the short type you find in newspapers and magazines. You may want to write a paragraph or two for each one, telling some history, a story, or interesting facts. Your *visual display* must focus on your *neighborhood*.

B. Write a *report* about your *hometown*. Include a short history of how and when it was "founded." You may also want to write about:
1. Important past events
2. The economy; how people make a living, local businesses, farming, industries, etc.
3. Population information
4. Community services: how many firefighters and police officers? Where are the hospitals?
5. Interesting people who live in your town
6. City celebrations or special events
7. The geographical setting
8. Weather
9. Places to visit in your town

This report should be a minimum of three pages.

V. PROJECT IDEAS

A. Produce a news feature as if you were a reporter/photographer doing a story for the local paper or better yet, the *National Geographic*. Write about the town and focus photographically on your neighborhood.

B. Interview "old-timers" to get ideas and stories about life in your town. Ask about the weather (floods, tornadoes, drought, blizzards, and so forth), important events, people who made news. Combine this report with a scrapbook of your neighborhood photographs.

C. You may want to have a theme for your photographs such as "Historical Buildings in My Neighborhood" and have them illustrate a report about architecture in your town. Perhaps your project could be titled "People from My Neighborhood"; photograph each person you interview and write a report consisting of short biographies and stories about your town.

D. Make the display look like pages from a family photo album and show personal things about the neighborhood such as your house, you and your friends playing a game, your next door neighbor, your favorite spot to sit and think, and the like. Include your hometown report in the front of the album.

VI. DUE DATES

A. Mid-Project Report: _____

B. Final Project: _____

VII. WRITTEN PERMISSION

My son/daughter_____
(Student's name)

has access to a camera. I am willing to buy a roll of 12-exposure color print film and pay to have it developed and printed.

_____

(Parent Signature)   (Date)

THE VIETNAM WAR
Student Assignment Sheet

I. INTRODUCTION

Wars are fought for many reasons: to protect a nation's interests, to expand territory, to defend a country from an aggressive neighbor, to force one country to think or behave like another, to gain influence and political power. The reasons that a government has for going to war have a lot to do with how much support it gets from its people. If the general population strongly opposes a war, it is very difficult for a government to continue conducting it.

The United States became involved in a war in Vietnam because our leaders were determined to stop the spread of communism in southeast Asia. Vietnam is a long, narrow country located south of China and due west of the Philippine Islands. North Vietnam, which bordered communist China, became independent of French colonial rule in 1954. So did South Vietnam. Under Ho Chi Minh, North Vietnam became a communist country which aggressively tried to spread communism to the south. The United States first tried to prevent the spread of communism into South Vietnam by sending American military supplies to support a weak, undemocratic government. When this didn't work, the United States sent its own army, which eventually numbered over 500,000 soldiers. Because of the type of war being fought, the unpopularity of the reasons for continuing the war, and the widespread belief that America should not be in Vietnam, the U.S. army was withdrawn in 1975. The Vietnam war was a controversial, divisive, and tragic period of American history, but one that should be studied and understood.

II. IDENTIFYING TOPICS (point III of the contract)

Use encyclopedias to identify at least ten topics that you could study about the Vietnam war. Choose *one* of these topics for your project. Here are some key terms that you can look up:

A. Vietnam war
B. Lyndon B. Johnson
C. Richard M. Nixon
D. Ho Chi Minh
E. Viet Cong
F. Saigon
G. Hanoi
H. The Tet Offensive
I. General William Westmoreland
J. Ngo Dinh Diem

III. FINDING SOURCES (point V of the contract)

Find five sources of information about your topic. You may include a person who fought in the Vietnam war as one of your sources. There are many encyclopedia references, library books, biographies, magazine articles, filmstrips, textbooks, and other materials available about the Vietnam war. You should have no difficulty locating enough sources of information to do this project.

IV. GENERAL REQUIREMENTS

A. Design a presentation that explains what you have learned.

B. You will be required to present your project to your teacher or to your class, and perhaps to other audiences.

V. PROJECT IDEA

Make a large wall map, or a tabletop relief map, and show where major battles and important events took place. Also show cities, towns, borders, and geographic features that played a role in the war:

A. Mekong River

B. Da Nang

C. Haiphong harbor

D. Saigon (now called Ho Chi Minh City)

E. Gulf of Tonkin

F. Hanoi

G. Ho Chi Minh Trail

H. 17th parallel

VI. DUE DATES

A. Mid-Project Report: _____

B. Final Project: _____

WOMEN IN HISTORY
Student Assignment Sheet

I. INTRODUCTION

Through the ages of history women have made major contributions to every area of human undertaking. Their efforts have often gone unnoticed or unacknowledged, though, because their accomplishments were overshadowed by men who were in positions of power and authority. The people who recorded history focused on the deeds of men, while women suffered from lack of recognition. Recently much attention has been given to the role played by women in the drama of human achievement and development. Have you heard of Sojourner Truth or Jane Addams or Isadora Duncan or Susan B. Anthony? How about Indira Ghandi or Elizabeth I or Mother Teresa? These were (or are) all important historical figures who made a lasting impression on the world. Studying about these women, or any of hundreds of others, will teach you about history, society, and culture; at the same time it will impress upon you the value of learning about women who contributed their talents and efforts to the world. You have a choice of many, many fascinating stories to investigate, and if you are careful in selecting a famous woman to study, you will enjoy this project very much.

II. IDENTIFYING TOPICS (point III of the contract)

Select ten women that you may be interested in studying. Choose *one* of these women for your project. Don't limit yourself to women that you have already heard of or know something about. Conduct an investigation to learn about women that you have not previously studied. A list of 75 women is provided with this project to help with topic selection. There are many others. If you are interested in a specific period of history, like colonial days, the American Civil War, or the Great Depression, look it up in encyclopedias and scan the articles for names of women that played important roles. Do the same if you are interested in a particular country such as France or England.

1. Abigail Adams
2. Gertrude Bell
3. Clare Boothe Luce
4. Jane Byrne
5. Empress Catherine the Great
6. Shirley Chisholm
7. Ch'iu Chin
8. Cleopatra
9. Bernadette Devlin
10. Queen Elizabeth I
11. Indira Gandhi
12. Queen Isabella of Spain
13. Mary Harris Jones
14. Golda Meir
15. Rosa Parks
16. Alice Paul
17. Eva Perón
18. Eleanor Roosevelt
19. Margaret Thatcher
20. Jane Addams
21. Susan B. Anthony
22. Carrie Chapman Catt
23. Helen Keller
24. Dorothea Dix
25. Maria Montessori
26. Lucy Stone
27. Sojourner Truth
28. Harriet Tubman
29. Catherine Booth
30. St. Joan of Arc
31. Mary Slessor
32. Mother Teresa
33. Louisa May Alcott

34. Charlotte Brontë
35. Elizabeth Barrett Browning
36. Agatha Christie
37. George Eliot
38. Anne Frank
39. Beatrix Potter
40. Harriet Beecher Stowe
41. Isadora Duncan
42. Mary Pickford
43. Dorothea Lange
44. Grandma Moses
45. Clara Barton
46. Marie Curie
47. Jane Goodall

48. Margaret Mead
49. Florence Nightingale
50. Dixy Lee Ray
51. Marie Tussaud
52. Amelia Earhart
53. Billie Jean King
54. Annie Oakley
55. Wilma Rudolph
56. Sacajawea
57. Coretta Scott King
58. Lady Bird Johnson
59. Sandra O'Connor
60. Barbara Walters
61. Carry Nation

62. Bella Abzug
63. Mildred Didrikson
64. Mary McLeod Bethune
65. Pocahontas
66. Sarah and Angelina Grimké
67. Nancy Reagan
68. Rosalyn Carter
69. Mary Queen of Scots
70. Margaret Chase Smith
71. Barbara Jordan
72. Beverly Sills
73. Betty Ford
74. Lucille Ball
75. Betsy Ross

III. FINDING SOURCES (point V of the contract)

Find five sources of information about the woman you have chosen to study. In addition to encyclopedias, there may be information in library books, biographies, magazine articles, filmstrips, textbooks, history books, and other materials. Ask your librarian for help.

IV. GENERAL REQUIREMENTS

A. Design a presentation that explains what you have learned.
B. You will be required to present the project to the teacher or to the class, and perhaps to other audiences.

V. PROJECT IDEAS

A. Write a biography.
   1. Date of birth and death
   2. Three or four major accomplishments
   3. Hometowns and other important places
   4. Family information
   5. Explanation of what role the woman played in history
   6. Whatever other information is available
B. Make a time line that shows events in the woman's life.
C. Make a mobile that shows the accomplishments of the woman, and some important dates and facts.
D. Make a mural about the woman's life: a visual biography.
E. Build a diorama with cardboard cutouts showing an important event from the person's life.

VI. DUE DATES

A. Mid-Project Report: _____

B. Final Project: _____

WORLD WAR II
Student Assignment Sheet

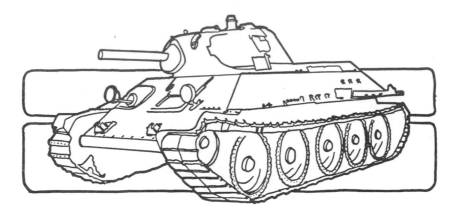

I. INTRODUCTION

World War II was a global conflict that involved most of the countries on earth. It was fought on land, in the air, and on the seas; battles were fought on three continents and on three oceans. The seeds for World War II were sown at the conclusion of World War I. The loser of the First World War, Germany, had to pay a steep price by disarming itself and paying large sums of money to the victors. The worldwide Great Depression that hit in the 1930s gave rise to desperation and anger in Germany. This atmosphere produced the man who led Germany to recovery and into World War II: Adolf Hitler.

There are *many* people in America who remember World War II. Your grandfather may have fought in it. The war was a battle for freedom in the world, and it raged for two years in Europe and China before Japan attacked Pearl Harbor on December 7, 1941. In Europe the war ended with the death of Adolf Hitler in May, 1945. On August 6, 1945 an atomic bomb was dropped by the United States on Hiroshima, Japan, and on August 9 an even stronger one was dropped on Nagasaki. On September 2, 1945, Japan signed a formal surrender and World War II was over.

World War II played a very large part in shaping the world we live in today. It resulted in Great Britain losing its empire, the United States gaining in power, the creation of the state of Israel, the development of the atomic bomb, and the division between "East" and "West" that runs through the middle of Europe. For the first time in history fully mechanized warfare was launched with gasoline engines: tanks, airplanes, submarines, battleships, trucks. It was an awesome, stupendous, terrible, frightening, deadly war, and a war that is truly fascinating to study, evaluate, and understand. Choose your topic carefully, and you will have a project that will prove to be interesting as well as educational.

II. IDENTIFYING TOPICS (point III of the contract)

Use encyclopedias to identify at least ten topics that you could study about World War II. Choose *one* of these topics for your project. Here are some key terms that you can look up:

A. World War II: European Theater
B. World War II: Pacific Theater
C. World War II: African Theater
D. Dwight Eisenhower
E. George Patton
F. Douglas MacArthur
G. Operation OVERLORD
H. Winston Churchill
I. Nazis
J. Pearl Harbor

III. FINDING SOURCES (point V of the contract)

Find five sources of information about your topic. In addition to encyclopedias, there are many library books, history books, textbooks, biographies, magazine articles, filmstrips, and other materials about World War II. There should be no difficulty locating enough sources of information to do this project.

IV. GENERAL REQUIREMENTS

A. Design a presentation that explains what you have learned.

B. You will be required to present the project to your teacher or to your class, and perhaps to other audiences.

V. PROJECT IDEAS

A. Choose an important battle and describe it.
1. Who were the generals?
2. Where did it occur? (Show it on a map!)
3. Describe each army and the moves it made.
4. Who won?
5. What was at stake?
6. Present any other information that you can find.

B. Make a time line of events that led up to and continued through the war.

C. Make a mobile that shows people who were involved in the Second World War or that describes important battles.

D. Make a mural that shows the major weapons that were used during the war, and which side developed and used each weapon.

E. Make a series of maps that show Axis strength, Allied strength, and army movements at various points during the war.

F. Choose one person and write his or her biography.

VI. DUE DATES

A. Mid-Project Report: _____

B. Final Project: _____

SOCIAL STUDIES OPEN HOUSE

Teacher Preview

Length of Project: 4 hours, plus 1 afternoon or evening
Level of Independence: Advanced
General Explanation:

The Social Studies Open House is designed to let students present their work to parents, relatives, friends, and students from other classes. It is a way of culminating a social studies curriculum so that all of the units, lessons, and projects coalesce into one final presentation by an entire class.

Goals:

1. To allow students an opportunity to display their knowledge and understanding of social studies.
2. To place emphasis on independent learning.
3. To provide a project that unifies the year's curriculum.

During This Project Students Will:

1. Choose areas of the curriculum they would like to present.
2. Develop presentations and displays.
3. Present their work to audiences of parents, teachers, and other students.

Skills: All of the skills on the Skills Chart may be incorporated and emphasized.
Handouts Provided: Any of the handouts in this book may be used.

PROJECT CALENDAR:

HOUR 1: _____	HOUR 2: _____	HOUR 3: _____
Introduction to the Open House. Discussion about different areas of the curriculum and how they could be presented to parents.	Students decide what they want to present and write descriptions of what their presentations will involve.	Presentation descriptions are turned in and discussed. STUDENTS TURN IN WORK
HOUR 4: _____	**HOUR 5:** _____	**HOUR 6:** _____
Dress rehearsal for the Social Studies Open House. NEED SPECIAL MATERIALS	For an afternoon or an evening students present examples of the kind of things they learned all year in the social studies class.	
HOUR 7: _____	**HOUR 8:** _____	**HOUR 9:** _____

Lesson Plans and Notes

HOUR 1: Introduce students to the idea of a Social Studies Open House that is designed to present the year's curriculum to parents and other interested people. Spend the hour discussing the various subjects that were covered during the year and ask students for their ideas on how to present those subjects to parents. Tell students to come to the next class prepared with at least three ideas for open house presentations, based upon the year's social studies curriculum.

HOUR 2: Spend this hour listing the ideas students have for open house presentations. Write each student's ideas on the board for easy reference when, at the end of the hour, you make the assignments. Try to give each student one of the three ideas he or she brought to class. Students are to write descriptions of their presentations for the next hour.

Notes:

- It is a good idea to bring some presentation ideas to class this hour, especially for areas of the curriculum that students may not choose. The Open House should cover all parts of the year if possible. Also, some students may quibble over a particularly choice idea that more than one person has thought of, and arbitration is more successful if there are alternatives to offer.

- Here are some presentation ideas, based upon this book:

  a. A "Who's in the News" presentation of famous people, with a bulletin board background. Students "introduce" these people to the audience.

  b A display of topical newspaper collages, with student presentations or group discussions; or, a display of divergent and convergent collages with a student explaining how the project was run.

  c. A collection of artifacts housed in a museum in the year 3000 A.D. Student guides explain what the artifacts show about life at the end of the twentieth century.

  d. A presentation of a class-made *Book of History,* a discussion of information from the book and an explanation of how the project was run.

  e. A "press conference" about the Soviet Union and its current relations with the rest of the world. Students make brief presentations and then answer questions from the audience.

  f. A demonstration of the 4-Across game and examples of coordinate mapping, along with a display of continent maps.

  g. A reading presentation: students read biographies of famous people to the audience. *Or,* dress up as a famous person and present an "autobiography" to the audience.

  h. A display of murals depicting scenes from early American history, with student presentations explaining what is being shown.

    i. Presentations on any or all of the 18 "Individualized Learning Projects."

    j. An explanation of independent learning skills and why they are impor-
       tant in a social studies class.

HOUR 3: Students describe their presentation ideas to the class, and they are discussed. Ideas that do not seem likely to work are revised. At the end of the hour students turn in their written presentation descriptions.

Note:

- A period of time (at *least* one week) should be provided between Hour 3 and Hour 4 for students to prepare their displays and presentations. Request that special material needs such as electrical outlets, podiums, projectors, screens, and chalkboards be handed in two or three days before Hour 4 is conducted.

HOUR 4: Dress rehearsal: students work on their presentations individually in different areas of the room, gymnasium, auditorium, or wherever the Social Studies Open House is to be held.

HOUR 5: Students make their presentations every fifteen or twenty minutes to small groups of parents who move from one presentation to another.

General Notes About This Project:

- The presentation ideas listed under Hour 2 all call for students to make oral presentations. There are many other options, some of which are provided here:

    a. A visual display of posters, models, charts, graphs, and reports

    b. A "hands-on" activity where guests follow simple instructions to create their own collages, scrapbooks, or time lines

    c. A slide show

    d. A video program

    e. A computer program

- It is a good idea to establish an "Information Bureau," consisting of three to four students, to send out special invitations to the Social Studies Open House, and to develop a directory that tells where each student in the class has his or her display. The directory can also give the times for presentations through the evening.

- An Open House is an excellent opportunity to transform projects that were taught at a basic level of independence into advanced projects. It may require little independence or use of higher level thinking skills to learn about who is in the news, for example, but to *teach others* about what has been learned is a different matter. Planning and presenting a lesson about current events is a highly individualized undertaking that requires higher level thinking.

Appendix

Teacher's Introduction to the Student Research Guide

Many of the projects in *Learning on Your Own!* require students to conduct research. Few children, however, possess the necessary skills to successfully complete this type of project. The research guide is designed to help them learn and practice some basic skills: how to locate, record, organize, and present information about topics they study. Even though the handouts in the guide are detailed, students will need some guidance and instructional support from you as they undertake their first research projects.

This Teacher's Introduction to the guide contains three forms that can be used to evaluate how well students do on (1) notecards, (2) posters, and (3) oral presentations. These are designed as optional evaluations that may be used with many projects in the book, regardless of subject or topic area.

Teaching a lesson on "how to use the library" is one type of instructional support you should give students to prepare them for research. Therefore, a "Typical Library Quiz" is also included in this Teacher's Introduction for you to give students after they have become acquainted with the library.

The Student Research Guide will be most useful to students if you spend some time explaining the following topics to your class.

1. *Library skills:* Use an example of a real library to explain how books and periodicals are categorized and where they are stored. Whatever library is most likely to be used by students should serve as a model. Cover these things in a library skills unit:

   a. The card catalog (handout provided)

   b. How to find a book from its call number (handout provided)

   c. The *Readers' Guide to Periodical Literature* and other periodical guides (handout provided)

   d. How to ask questions and use librarians as helpful resources

   e. Other kinds of information and services offered by libraries

2. *Notecards and bibliographies:* Provide a variety of examples of properly made notecards and bibliographies for students to use as models. (Reference handout provided.) Explain how to use a numbering system to cross-reference a set of notecards with a bibliography. Spend enough time on bibliographies to ensure

that students know how to write them for the most common sources (books, magazines, encyclopedias, and newspapers).

3. *The Readers' Guide to Periodical Literature*: You can teach students how to use this valuable resource before they ever go to a library. Contact the librarian and ask for old monthly *RGPL* discards. Collect them until you have at least one for every student in the room. During your library skills unit pass the guides out and write ten topics on the board, for example:

a. The president of the United States
b. The automobile industry
c. Basketball (or football, baseball, hockey, and so on)
d. Ballet
e. Acid rain
f. Poland
g. Israel
h. Martin Luther King, Jr.
i. Satellites
j. Agriculture

Tell students to choose five topics, find at least one article about each and properly record the title of the article, the author of the article, the name of the magazine, its volume number, the pages on which it can be found, and the date it was published.

4. *Common sources of information:* Encourage students to make extensive use of encyclopedias, magazines such as *National Geographic, Junior Scholastic, Newsweek* and others that are readily available, textbooks and workbooks, materials from home, and whatever other sources are in the classroom or school library. Always require that adequate information from these common sources be available before allowing a research project to begin.

The Student Research Guide is primarily a series of handouts. You may want to give them to students as a complete booklet or hand them out individually to be used with separate, specific research lessons. The research guide is supplied as an aid to help students tackle projects that require research and independent work. The handouts *supplement* what is being taught in the projects, and they provide excellent reference materials for independent learning.

© 1987 by The Center for Applied Research in Education, Inc.

Name _____ Date _____

NOTECARD EVALUATION

Below are ten areas for which your notecards have been evaluated. This breakdown of your final score, which is at the bottom of the sheet, indicates the areas where improvement is needed and where you have done well.

	EXCELLENT (10 pts.)	VERY GOOD (9 pts.)	GOOD (7 pts.)	FAIR (6 pts.)	POOR (4 pts.)	NOT DONE OR INCOMPLETE (0 pts.)
1. Bibliography	____	____	____	____	____	____
2. Reference between notecards and bibliography	____	____	____	____	____	____
3. Headings and subheadings	____	____	____	____	____	____
4. Organizing information onto cards so it can be understood and used later without confusion: numbering system	____	____	____	____	____	____
5. Neatness (If reading or use of the cards is made difficult because of sloppy writing, "POOR" will be checked.)	____	____	____	____	____	____
6. Recording meaningful information (Everything recorded on notecards should relate directly to your topic.)	____	____	____	____	____	____
7. Spelling	____	____	____	____	____	____
8. Accuracy of information	____	____	____	____	____	____
9. Quantity (Did you do as much work as you were supposed to, or should have, to complete the project?)	____	____	____	____	____	____
10. Information properly recorded (Facts must be brief and understandable. It is best to condense information into concise statements. Entire paragraphs should not be copied onto notecards. Direct quotes must be identified.)	____	____	____	____	____	____

FINAL SCORE _____ (100 possible)

COMMENTS _____

_____

Name _____ Date _____

POSTER EVALUATION

Below are ten areas for which your poster has been evaluated. This breakdown of your final score, which is at the bottom of the sheet, indicates the areas where improvement is needed and where you have done well.

	EXCELLENT (10 pts.)	VERY GOOD (9 pts.)	GOOD (7 pts.)	FAIR (6 pts.)	POOR (4 pts.)	NOT DONE OR INCOMPLETE (0 pts.)
1. Facts which your poster teaches (at least twenty)	_____	_____	_____	_____	_____	_____
2. Poster "goes along with" your written report	_____	_____	_____	_____	_____	_____
3. Visual impact: use of color, headings, and lettering	_____	_____	_____	_____	_____	_____
4. Drawings (at least one)	_____	_____	_____	_____	_____	_____
5. Pictures, articles, headlines, quotes, charts, graphs, diagrams, explanations, and so forth	_____	_____	_____	_____	_____	_____
6. Organization of material	_____	_____	_____	_____	_____	_____
7. Neatness	_____	_____	_____	_____	_____	_____
8. Spelling, grammar, writing skills	_____	_____	_____	_____	_____	_____
9. Accurate information	_____	_____	_____	_____	_____	_____
10. Specific topic; proper material (Did you do a good job of presenting your topic?)	_____	_____	_____	_____	_____	_____

FINAL SCORE _____ (100 possible)

COMMENTS _____

_____

_____

Name _____ Date _____

ORAL PRESENTATION EVALUATION

This form shows how your oral presentation has been evaluated. It indicates areas where improvement is needed and where you have done well.

Topic _____

I. Presentation (50 points possible)

    A. Eye contact.   3 pts. _____
    B. Voice projection.   3 pts. _____
    C. Use of the English language.   3 pts. _____
    D. Inflection.   3 pts. _____
    E. Articulation.   3 pts. _____
    F. Posture.   3 pts. _____
    G. Use of hands.   3 pts. _____
    H. Appropriate vocabulary.   3 pts. _____
    I. Accurate information.   10 pts. _____
    J. Information is easy to understand.   3 pts. _____
    K. Enough information.   3 pts. _____
    L. Information relates to topic.   3 pts. _____
    M. Effort.   7 pts. _____

          Subtotal _____

II. Visual or Extra Materials (30 points possible)

    A. Information is easy to understand.   3 pts. _____
    B. Information relates to the oral report.   3 pts. _____
    C. Information is current.   3 pts. _____
    D. Information is accurate.   3 pts. _____
    E. Enough information.   3 pts. _____
    F. Neatness.   3 pts. _____
    G. Spelling.   3 pts. _____
    H. Artistic effort.   3 pts. _____
    I. Research effort.   3 pts. _____
    J. Appropriate vocabulary.   3 pts. _____

          Subtotal _____

III. Question-Answer Period (20 points possible)

    A. Confidence in knowledge of topic.   3 pts. _____
    B. Ability to answer reasonable questions.   3 pts. _____
    C. Answers are accurate.   3 pts. _____
    D. Student is willing to admit limits of knowledge or understanding such as "I don't know."   2 pts. _____
    E. Answers are brief.   3 pts. _____
    F. Student exhibits ability to infer or hypothesize an answer from available information.   3 pts. _____
    G. Student appears to have put effort into learning about this topic.   3 pts. _____

          Subtotal _____

          TOTAL (100 pts. possible) _____

COMMENTS _____

Name _____ Date _____

TYPICAL LIBRARY QUIZ

How well do you know the library? Answer these questions and find out.

1. List four kinds of information you can find on a card in the card catalog:

   a. _____

   b. _____

   c. _____

   d. _____

2. What does "jB" tell you about a book when it precedes the call number?

   _____

3. What does "jR" tell you about a book when it precedes the call number?

   _____

4. Suppose you are writing a report about polar bears. You look up "polar bears" in the card catalog but find only a few sources. What would you look under next?

   _____

5. If you are looking for a book with the call number j598.132/D43, would you find it before or after j598.2/D42?

   _____

6. If you are looking for "G-men" in the card catalog, you may find a card that says "G-men, see U.S. Federal Bureau of Investigation." Where would you look next?

   _____

7. List these call numbers in the order that they would be found on the shelf:

   j973.15   j973.35   j973.3   j973
   Ad32   Ab24   Cy31   Ad55

   a. _____   c. _____

   b. _____   d. _____

8. Books of fiction are shelved alphabetically by _____.

9. Biographies are shelved alphabetically by _____.

10. What do the words or letters on the front of a card catalog drawer tell you? (example: Istanbul—jets)

_____

11. How long can books be checked out of the library?

_____

12. If the book you are looking for is not on the shelf, what should you do?

_____

13. Where would you go to find a listing of all the magazines your library subscribes to? (Circle the correct answer.)

    a. Card catalog   d. Young adults

    b. History and travel   e. *Readers' Guide to Periodical Literature*

    c. Information desk

14. For *current* information, where should you check first?

    a. Encyclopedia   c. Card Catalog

    b. *Readers' Guide to*   d. Book shelves
       Periodical Literature   e. Reference shelves

15. Below is an excerpt from the *Readers' Guide to Periodical Literature*. Look it over and then answer the questions:

         The real cost of a car. S. Porter, il Ladies Home J. 99:58 Je '82

    a. What is the title of the article? _____

    b. Who wrote the article? _____

    c. What month and year was the article published? _____

    d. What magazine published the article? _____

    e. In what volume of the magazine was the article published? _____

    f. On what page can the article be found? _____

    g. Where in the library would you be most likely to find this article?

_____

Student Research Guide

STUDENT RESEARCH GUIDE

Research is the process you go through to find information about a topic that interests you. This guide explains some basic tools needed to find and record information. It gives advice about how to conduct a research project and also provides many suggestions for developing a *presentation* of the topic.

A list of skills that you will use during research projects includes finding resources, choosing topics, writing and note taking, summarizing, organizing ideas, scanning, planning, and interpreting data. This guide will help in many of these areas.

Of course, the real quality of a project is determined by the personal characteristics you bring to it—things like patience, motivation, accuracy, neatness, humor, persistence, and creativity. There are no handouts in the Student Research Guide that teach these things, but they are perhaps the most essential ingredients of a successful project.

Your Research Guide contains the following handouts:

"Outlining"

"Bibliographies"

"Notecards and Bibliographies"

"Sending for Information"

"The Dewey Decimal Classification System"

"The Card Catalog"

"The Readers' Guide to Periodical Literature"

"Choosing a Subject"

"Audio-Visual and Written Information Guides"

"Where to Go or Write for Information"

"Project Fact Sheet"

"Project Fact Sheet: Example"

"Poster Display Sheet"

"Things to Check Before Giving Your Presentation"

"Visual Aids for the Oral Presentation"

"Things to Remember When Presenting Your Project"

"Daily Log"

"Blank Skills Chart"

OUTLINING

I. Outlining is like classification: it sorts ideas and facts into categories or like-groups. This is an important skill to have when you are conducting a research project because you must organize information before you can use it.

II. Outlining separates main ideas from details in two ways:
   A. By symbols
      1. Alternating letters and numbers
      2. Same symbol = same importance
   B. By indentation
      1. Indent more with each subheading
      2. Same margin = same importance

I.
II.
   A.
   B.
      1.
      2.
         a)
         b)
            (1)
            (2)

III. It is very important to understand that every item in an outline can be expanded with additional research or new information. The outline below is incomplete, but it shows how to use symbols and indentation to organize facts and ideas into a logical order. When you make an outline, leave plenty of room between lines so additional ideas can be included later. Think of ways to expand this outline:

EXAMPLE: My Autobiography

I. Early years

   A. Birth
      1. Place
      2. Date
      3. Time
      4. Other details

   B. Family
      1. Father
      2. Mother
      3. Brothers and sisters
      4. Other members of the extended family
      5. Other important adults in your life

C. First home
   1. Location and description
      a) address
      b) type of house
      c) color
      d) trees in yard
         (1) tall maple in back
         (2) two cherries in front
         (3) giant oak in side yard
            (a) rope swing
            (b) tree house
            (c) shade
               i. summer afternoon naps
               ii. lemonade stand three summers ago
   2. Neighborhood
   3. Experiences

II. School years

   A. School or schools attended
      1. School name and description
      2. Favorite teacher(s)
      3. Favorite subject(s)
   B. Significant experiences
      1. Vacations
      2. Births
      3. Deaths
      4. Adventures
      5. Ideas and beliefs
   C. Friends

III. Present

   A. Residence

   B. Family

   C. School

   D. Hobbies and interests

   E. Friends

IV. Future

   A. Education

   B. Career

   C. Personal goals

   D. Vacations—trips

   E. Family

BIBLIOGRAPHIES

A bibliography is a standard method for recording where information came from. It is important to be able to prove that research came from legitimate sources. Use the following forms when recording information for bibliographies:

I. When working with a book:

A. Author's last name first
B. Full title underlined
C. Place of publication
D. Date of publication
E. Publisher
F. Page(s)

NOTECARD FORM:

Galbraith, John K.
<u>The Affluent Society</u>
Boston
1966
Houghton Mifflin
76

STANDARD FORM:

Galbraith, John K. <u>The Affluent Society</u>. Boston: Houghton Mifflin, 1966; 76.

II. When working with a periodical:

A. Author's last name first
B. Full article title in quotes
C. Name of periodical underlined
D. Volume number
E. Date in parentheses
F. Page(s)

NOTECARD FORM:

Lippman, Walter
"Cuba and the Nuclear Race"
<u>Atlantic</u>
211
(Feb. 1963)
55–58

STANDARD FORM:

Lippmann, Walter. "Cuba and the Nuclear Race." <u>Atlantic</u> 211 (February 1963): 55–58.

III. When working with newspaper articles:

    A. Author's last name first
    B. Full article title in quotes

    C. Name of paper underlined
    D. Date
    E. Section (some papers are not divided into sections)
    F. Page

NOTECARD FORM:

May, Clifford D.
"Campus Report: Computers In, Typewriters Out"
The New York Times
May 12, 1986

28

STANDARD FORM:

May, Clifford D. "Campus Report: Computers In, Typewriters Out," The New York Times, May 12, 1986, p. 28.

IV. When working with an encyclopedia:

    A. Author's last name first
    B. Full title of article in quotes
    C. Name of encyclopedia underlined
    D. Date of publication in parentheses
    E. Volume number
    F. Page(s)

NOTECARD FORM:

Clutz, Donald G.
"Television"
Encyclopaedia Britannica
(1963)
21
910

STANDARD FORM:

Clutz, Donald G. "Television," Encyclopaedia Britannica (1963), 21, 910.

NOTECARDS AND BIBLIOGRAPHIES

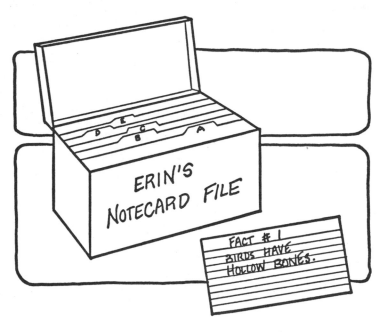

Notecards are used to record and collect information. Bibliography cards are used to tell where the information came from. Once information is gathered about a topic, notecards become the main tool for writing a report. Since each notecard contains a separate idea, you can arrange and rearrange these ideas into an order that becomes an outline for your report. If more information is needed about a particular fact, or, if something needs to be clarified, bibliography cards will tell which source to go to.

Each card should be numbered. It is *very* important that each notecard have a bibliography card number to tell where each fact came from. For example, if you study a unit called "Ecology" in science class, you could do a project about air pollution. Suppose you found information about air pollution in a book titled *Environmental Pollution*—you would make one bibliography card for this source, regardless of how many facts you obtained from it. If this book was the fifth source you used, the bibliography card for it would be numbered "5" in the upper right.

Now, suppose that the chapter on air pollution has four facts, or pieces of information, that you want to use. Make four notecards, each with a unit or course title at the top ("Ecology") and the topic being studied on the next line ("air pollution"). Number these cards in the upper right-hand corner, continuing the numbers from the last card of your fourth source. In other words, if you have 17 notecards from your first four sources, the next card you make will be number 18.

Next, tell where you found the information on each notecard. Do this by writing "see bibliography card 5" at the bottom right of each of these four notecards. This clearly shows that you have to look at bibliography card number five to find out where the information came from.

Remember to put only one important fact on each notecard. Don't copy long passages from sources onto notecards; condense information into easily stated facts. If a quote is included in your report, however, it *should* be recorded word for word. Also, if you record your bibliography on notebook paper instead of notecards, each source must still be numbered.

Here is a sample notecard:

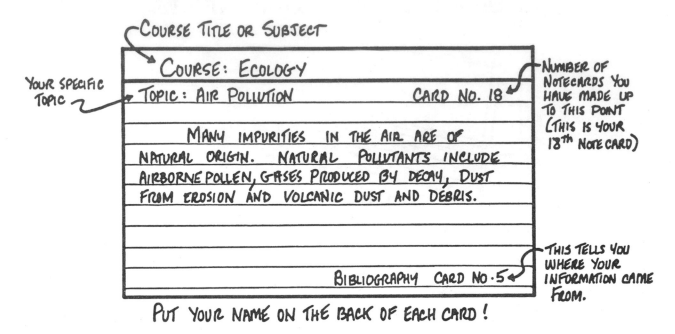

Course Title or Subject

Your specific topic

Course: Ecology

Topic: Air Pollution   Card No. 18

Number of notecards you have made up to this point (this is your 18th notecard)

Many impurities in the air are of natural origin. Natural pollutants include airborne pollen, gases produced by decay, dust from erosion and volcanic dust and debris.

Bibliography Card No. 5

This tells you where your information came from.

Put your name on the back of each card!

If you are required to record your bibliography on notecards, here is a sample bibliography card:

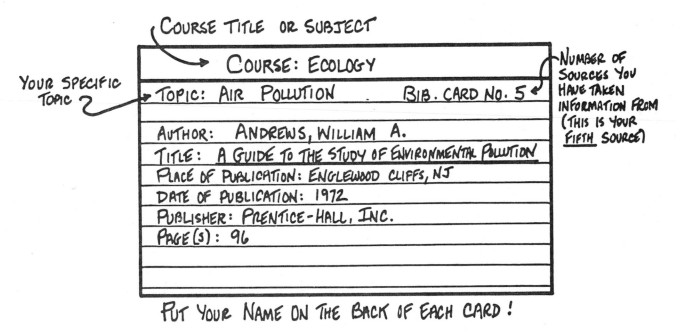

Course Title or Subject

Your specific topic

Course: Ecology

Topic: Air Pollution   Bib. Card No. 5

Number of sources you have taken information from (this is your fifth source)

Author: Andrews, William A.
Title: A Guide to the Study of Environmental Pollution
Place of Publication: Englewood Cliffs, NJ
Date of Publication: 1972
Publisher: Prentice-Hall, Inc.
Page(s): 96

Put your name on the back of each card!

SENDING FOR INFORMATION

There are times when sending a letter is the best way to obtain information about a research topic. Unfortunately, many people write letters hastily. They don't take time to explain themselves clearly or else they come across sounding unprofessional and insincere. You should learn how to write a good letter so that, when confronted with a difficult project, you can get help from others. Study the outline below. It explains why letter writing is a useful research skill and what components should be included in the letters you write. Examples of two letter styles are provided.

I. Reasons for sending a letter:

   A. To obtain up-to-date information.

   B. To make contact with experts or specific organizations.

   C. To get specialized or technical information.

   D. To ask for opinions and advice.

   E. To ask for suggestions of other places to look for information about the topic.

   F. To ask for free materials.

   G. To send special questions to authorities in the field you are studying.

II. Parts of a letter

A. Heading:	*Your* return address at the top of the letter, and the date right below your address.
B. Inside address:	The address of the person or organization to whom you are sending the letter.
C. Salutation:	Begin your letter with a salutation to the person you are sending it to: Dear Mr. Wilson; Dear Miss Goode; Dear Mrs. Smith; Dear Ms. Jones; Dear Sir.
D. Body:	Introduce yourself, explain your project, and ask for whatever assistance you are seeking. Be concise and clear in your writing; don't make someone guess what you want.
E. Complimentary close:	Show your respect by thanking the person to whom you have sent your letter for whatever help he or she can provide. Your letter might end like this:

"…I appreciate any advice or information you can offer to help me with my project.
Thank you."

Sincerely,

John Jones

F. Signature	Sign your name at the bottom of the letter, beneath the complimentary close.

Example of the "Block Letter" Style

John Jones
1532 Hill Street
Bridgeton, TX 75588

March 16, 19XX

Dr. David Adamson
Entomological Society
113 Geneva Road
Fair Ridge, OH 45289

Dear Dr. Adamson:

I am an eighth-grade student at Bridgeton Middle School, and we are doing a science project on insects. I am studying the praying mantis, and I have three questions that I can't find answers to from my research. I thought maybe you could help me.

I have enclosed a self-addressed, stamped envelope for your convenience. Here are my questions:

1. By what other names are praying mantises known?
2. How many species are there?
3. Can young praying mantises fly?

I appreciate any information you can provide about these questions. Thank you.

Sincerely,

John Jones

John Jones

Example of a "Modified Block Letter" Style

Dr. David Adamson
Entomological Society
113 Geneva Road
Fair Ridge, OH 45289

March 22, 19XX

John Jones
1532 Hill Street
Bridgeton, TX 75588

Dear John,

I received your letter of March 16, and I am glad to help you. Here are my answers to your questions:

1. The praying mantis is also known by these names: rearhorse, mule killer, devil's horse, and soothsayer.

2. There are 20 species of praying mantis. The European mantis is well established in the eastern U.S., and the Chinese mantis has also established itself in the eastern states.

3. One female lays up to 1,000 eggs in the fall, which hatch in May or June. The young cannot fly; they grow slowly, acquiring wings and maturity in August. When mature, four well-developed wings allow slow, extended flight.

I hope this information helps you in your research work. By the way, thank you for enclosing a stamped envelope—I appreciate that. If I can be of further assistance, please let me know.

Sincerely,

David Adamson, M.D.

Dr. David Adamson

DEWEY DECIMAL CLASSIFICATION SYSTEM

1. The Dewey Decimal Classification System arranges all knowledge into ten "classes" numbered 0 through 9. Libraries use this system to assign a "call number" to every book in the building. A call number is simply an identification number that tells where a book is located in the library.

   (000) 0—Generalities
   (100) 1—Philosophy and related disciplines
   (200) 2—Religion
   (300) 3—The social sciences
   (400) 4—Language
   (500) 5—Pure sciences
   (600) 6—Technology (applied sciences)
   (700) 7—The arts
   (800) 8—Literature and rhetoric
   (900) 9—General geography, history, and so forth

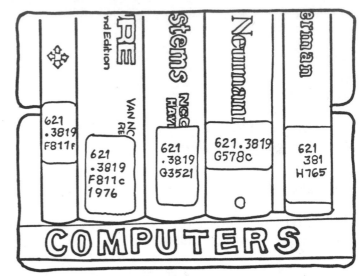

2. Each *class*, with the use of a three-digit number, is divided into ten subclasses (divisions) with the first division (600–609) set aside for the general works on the entire class. For example, 600–649:

   600–609 is given over to *general works* on the applied sciences
   610–619 to the medical sciences
   620–629 to engineering and applied operations
   630–639 to agriculture and agricultural industries
   640–649 to domestic arts and sciences

3. Each division is separated into ten subclasses or *"sections"* with the first *"section"* (630) devoted to the general works on the entire *division*. For example:

   630 is assigned to agriculture and agricultural industries in general
   631 to farming activities
   632 to plant diseases and pests and their control
   633 to production of field crops
   636 to livestock and domestic animals, etc.

4. Further subdividing is made by following the three-digit number with a decimal point and as many more digits as is necessary. For example, 631 farming is divided into

   631.2 for farm structures
   631.3 for farm tools, machinery, appliances
   631.5 for crop production

5. In summary, every book in a library is assigned a call number based upon the Dewey Decimal Classification System. All library books are stored on shelves according to their numbers, making them easy to find.

6. To locate a book in the library follow these steps:
   a. Use the card catalog to find the call number of a book in which you are interested. Books are cataloged by author, title, and subject.
   b. Record the call number, usually recorded in the upper left-hand corner of the card. If your library uses a computerized catalog system, ask a librarian for assistance in locating the call number.
   c. Refer to the first three numbers of the call number to determine in which section of the library your book can be found.
   d. Once you have found this section of the library, use the rest of the call number to locate the book on the shelf.

Name _____ Date _____

THE CARD CATALOG

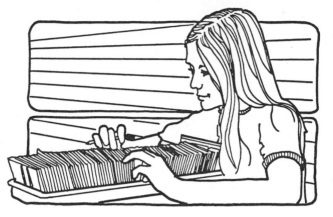

The card catalog is usually the first place you would go to look for a book in the library. The cards in the card catalog are arranged alphabetically by subject, author, and title. The card below is a "subject" card, filed under "inventors." The same book could be found if you looked under "Manchester, Harland Frank" (along with any other books Mr. Manchester has written) or *Trailblazers of Technology* (the title of the book).

Once you find the card that best fits your needs, the most important piece of information is the "call number" in the upper left-hand corner. This number tells you where to find the book in the library. In trying to decide which book to look up, you may refer to various pieces of information found on every catalog card. This information includes

1. Call number
2. Subject
3. Author
4. Author's birth date
5. Title
6. Brief description
7. Illustrator (if there is only one)

8. Location of publisher (city)
9. Publisher
10. Date of publication
11. Number of pages
12. Whether or not the book is illustrated
13. Size of the book

Here is a sample card:

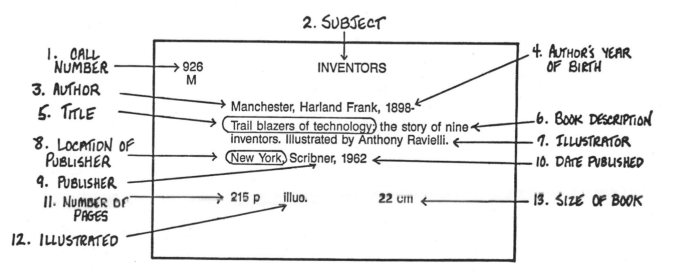

READERS' GUIDE TO PERIODICAL LITERATURE

The *Readers' Guide to Periodical Literature* is an extremely useful tool. You can find magazine articles about current topics from as recent as one or two months ago. You can also find articles that were written fifteen, twenty, or fifty years ago. Subject and author headings are arranged alphabetically in the *Guide*. Articles are arranged alphabetically under each heading.

When a promising reference is found, first determine how to locate the magazine that published the article. Does the library subscribe to the magazine? Is it a current issue? (Usually issues for the past twelve months will be available in the periodical reading section of the library.) Are old issues recorded on microfilm, or are they bound and placed in a special area of the library? When you find an article you want to read, record the following on a piece of paper. Then you or a librarian, if necessary, can locate the magazine from its file area.

The elements in each entry are

1. Title of the article
2. Author's name
3. Name of the magazine
4. Volume number
5. Pages on which the article can be found
6. Date of publication

The following is a section from the *Readers' Guide to Periodical Literature:*

Atomic bombs
           History
    See also
  Hiroshima (Japan)
          Physiological effects
    See Radiation—Physiological effects
          Testing
    See Atomic weapons—Testing
Atomic energy *See* Atomic power
Atomic energy industry *See* Atomic power industry
Atomic facilities *See* Nuclear facilities
Atomic fuels *See* Nuclear fuels
Atomic power
    See also
  Anti-nuclear movement
  Nuclear fuels
          Economic aspects
    See also
  Atomic power industry
          Laws and regulations
    See also
  Radioactive waste disposal—Laws and regulations
  Mixed rulings on nuclear power [Supreme Court decisions]
    R. Sandler. *Environment* 25:2-3 Jl/Ag '83
          Germany (West)
    See also
  Anti-nuclear movement—Germany (West)

Atomic power industry
   See also
   Computers—Atomic power industry use
   Reactor fuel reprocessing
   Washington Public Power Supply System
      Export-import trade
   Firing spotlights plutonium exports [R. Hesketh's claim
     that plutonium produced in Great Britain's civilian
     reactors has been used in U.S. weapons manufacture]
     D. Dickson. *Science* 221:245 Jl 15 '83
      Laws and regulations
   See Atomic power—Laws and regulations
      Public relations
   Atom and Eve [nuclear acceptance campaign geared to
     women] L. Nelson. il *Progressive* 47:32-4 Jl '83
      United States
   See Atomic power industry
Atomic power plants
      Economic aspects
   The bankruptcy of public power [Washington Public Power
     Supply System debacle] *Nat'l Rev* 35:982-3 Ag 19 '83
   Money meltdown [Washington Public Power Supply
     System default] S. Ridley. *New Repub* 189:11-13 Ag
     29 '83
   When billions in bonds go bust [default of Washington
     Public Power Supply System] *U S News World Rep*
     95:7 Ag 8 '83
   Whoops! A $2 billion blunder. C. P. Alexander. il *Time*
     122:50-2 Ag 8 '83
   The Whoops bubble bursts. H. Anderson. il *Newsweek*
     102:61-2 Ag 8 '83
      Laws and regulations
   See Atomic power—Laws and regulations
      Safety devices and measures
   Computers to supervise nuke plants. *Sci Dig* 91:27 Jl
     '83
Atomic research
   Pseudo-QCD [discussion of January 1983 article. A look
     at the future of particle physics] B. G. Levi. *Phys*
     Today 36:98+ Jl '83

Suppose you are studying atomic power; specifically, you want to find out about the costs of building and operating atomic power plants. By looking through a *Readers' Guide*, you will find many articles published about atomic power. From the example provided you can see that "atomic bombs" is at the top of the list of atomic topics, followed by atomic energy, atomic energy industry, atomic facilities, atomic fuels, atomic power, atomic power industry, atomic power plants, and atomic research. There, under "Atomic power plants—Economic aspects," is a collection of five articles that could be useful to you. Look at the fourth one:

Whoops! A $2 billion blunder. C.P. Alexander. il *Time* 122:50-2 Ag 8 '83

1. Title: "Whoops! A $2 Billion Blunder"
2. Author: C.P. Alexander
3. il: this article is illustrated with photographs or drawings
4. Magazine: *Time*
5. Volume: 122
6. Page(s): 50-52
7. Date: August 8, 1983

The *Readers' Guide to Periodical Literature* makes use of abbreviations for months of the year, magazine names, and other pieces of important information. For example, "Bet Hom & Gard" is *Better Homes and Gardens* and "bi-m" means a magazine is published bimonthly. Be sure to refer to the first few pages of the *Readers' Guide* for a complete list of all the abbreviations used.

CHOOSING A SUBJECT

The first step in any research project is choosing something to study. This requires some thought and decision making. This handout provides several guidelines that will help you select a subject.

1. Choose a subject that you are already interested in or that you would like to know more about.

2. Choose a subject that will meet the needs or requirements as outlined by the teacher:
   a. Listen for suggestions from the teacher.
   b. Be alert to ideas that come from class discussion.
   c. Talk to friends and parents about things you can study and learn.

3. A good rule by the Roman poet Horace: "Choose a subject, ye who write, suited to your strength." This means pick a subject you can understand, not one in which you will become bogged down, lost, or disinterested.

4. The encyclopedia should serve as a tool for choosing the right subject and narrowing it down so you can handle it:
   a. It gives the general areas of the subject.
   b. It identifies specific topics related to your subject.
   c. It is written simply enough to understand without hours of study.

5. Before you commit yourself to a subject, check to make sure there is some information available. There is nothing more frustrating than starting a project that cannot be finished because there are no books, magazines, filmstrips, newspapers, journals, experts, or even libraries that have enough information.

6. Once you have chosen a subject, write down a series of questions to which you want to find answers. Write as many as you can think of. These questions will help direct your research.

© 1987 by The Center for Applied Research in Education, Inc.

Name _____ Date _____

AUDIO-VISUAL AND WRITTEN INFORMATION GUIDES

DIRECTIONS: The following list shows some of the places where information can be found. When you begin your first project, go down column one and put a checkmark in the box next to each place you *might* be able to find information. When you *do* find information, fill in the appropriate box on the chart with your pencil. Do this for your first five research projects.

	PROJECT NUMBER				
	1	2	3	4	5
Almanacs					
Atlases					
Bibliographies					
Biographies					
Charts and graphs					
Dictionaries					
Encyclopedias					
Films					
Filmstrips					
Historical stories					
Indexes to free material					
Letters					
Library card catalog					
Magazines					
Maps					
Microfilm					
Newspapers					
Pictures					
Readers' Guide to Periodical Literature					
Records					
Tapes					
Textbooks					
Vertical files					
Other: _____					
_____					

Name _____ Date _____

WHERE TO GO OR WRITE FOR INFORMATION

DIRECTIONS: Before you start your project put a checkmark in the box next to each place you could go or write to get information. When you *do* get information, fill in the appropriate box.

PROJECT NUMBER

	1	2	3	4	5
Chambers of Commerce					
Churches					
City officials					
Companies					
Embassies					
Experts					
Factories					
Federal agencies					
Historical societies					
Hobbyists					
Librarians					
Libraries					
Ministers					
Museums					
Newspaper office/employee					
Organizations (club, societies)					
Professionals					
Research laboratories					
State agencies					
Teachers					
Travel agencies					
Universities					
Zoos					
Friends					
Home (books, magazines, etc.)					
Other: _____					
_____					

Name _____ Date _____

PROJECT FACT SHEET

One of the most difficult parts of any project is getting started. Use the "Project Fact Sheet" to begin recording information that will be included in a presentation or report. A sample of a completed "Project Fact Sheet" is shown on the next page.

My topic is _____

and these are the facts I am going to teach the rest of the class:

1. _____
2. _____
3. _____
4. _____
5. _____
6. _____
7. _____
8. _____
9. _____
10. _____
11. _____
12. _____
13. _____
14. _____
15. _____
16. _____
17. _____
18. _____
19. _____
20. _____

PROJECT FACT SHEET: Example

This sample fact sheet about humpback whales shows how to write out information that is to be included in a presentation.

My topic is <u>Humpback Whales,</u> and these are the facts I am going to teach the rest of the class:

1. Humpback whales spend six months in the South Pacific.
2. Humpback whales sing a strange song that seems to be some sort of communication.
3. Humpback whales sing only when they are in the South Pacific.
4. Humpback whales do not eat when they are in the South Pacific.
5. Humpback whales travel to an arctic Alaskan bay to feed.
6. A humpback whale has a brain that is five times larger than a human brain.
7. The invention of the explosive harpoon gun and the steam engine made full-scale hunting of the humpback whale possible.
8. Humpback whales show great devotion to one another; this is best displayed by the relationship between a mother and her young.
9. A young whale is called a "calf."
10. The humpback whale eats krill, which makes it a carnivorous mammal.
11. (This list is extended to whatever the project outline requires.)

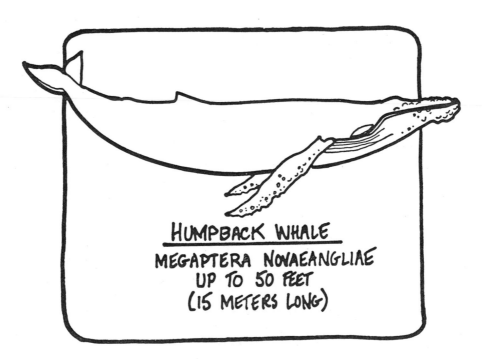

HUMPBACK WHALE
MEGAPTERA NOVAEANGLIAE
UP TO 50 FEET
(15 METERS LONG)

POSTER DISPLAY SHEET

Use the guidelines on this handout if you are required to make a poster for a research project.

1. Present or "teach" at least twenty facts about your topic on the poster. These facts should be recorded on notecards.

2. The poster should be made to go with the written report so that they can be used together when you make a presentation.

3. Include at least one of your own drawings on it.

4. The poster can also have other pictures, magazine articles, newspaper headlines, quotes from books, charts, graphs, illustrations, explanations, diagrams, captions, and so forth.

5. Organize all of the material on the poster so that it is easy to understand. This is very important when making a top-quality poster. Give your poster visual impact by using colorful designs, bold headings, and a catchy title.

6. Writing must be neat! Use parallel guidelines and pencil words in lightly before going over them with marker.

7. Check spelling, grammar, capitalization, punctuation, and sentences to be sure they are correct.

8. Every bit of information you use must be accurate. *Do not make anything up!*

9. Your poster should be about a very specific topic. Don't throw everything you can find onto it. Be selective and use only material that contributes favorably to the project.

10. OPTIONAL: Write five questions that can be answered by studying your poster. These questions should be attached to the poster.

Name _____ Date _____

THINGS TO CHECK BEFORE GIVING YOUR PRESENTATION

DIRECTIONS: After practicing your presentation at home one time, write "yes" or "no" in the boxes below to help determine which areas need more work. The purpose of this checklist is to help put *quality* into your presentation. Use it wisely and be honest. If something needs more time and effort, be willing to admit it and work to improve what you have done.

PROJECT NUMBER

	1	2	3	4	5
Have I done enough research?					
Is everything spelled correctly?					
Did I use neat handwriting?					
Is everything in my visual display labeled?					
Do all my pictures have captions?					
Is my visual display neat and attractive?					
Did I use colors in a pleasing way?					
Did I do my best artwork?					
Does my oral report need more practice?					
Do I know all the words in my report?					
Is it easy to understand what I have written?					
Is my report informative?					
Is my visual display informative?					
Do I understand the information I will present?					
Did I choose interesting and different presentation methods?					
Have I decided how I will display my visual materials during my presentation?					
Am I ready to answer questions about my subject?					
Did I follow the project directions or outline?					
Does my presentation stick to my subject?					
Is this my best work?					

Name _____ Date _____

VISUAL AIDS FOR THE ORAL PRESENTATION

DIRECTIONS: Making your report interesting is very important. Besides hearing what you have to say, the audience likes to see examples of what you've done. There are many ways to use visual aids during a presentation. This list provides some suggestions. First, check the items that you think you *could* use. Later, fill in the ones you actually *did* use.

	PROJECT NUMBER				
	1	2	3	4	5
Chalkboard					
Charts					
Clippings					
Diagrams					
Dioramas					
Film (slides)					
Filmstrips					
Guest speakers					
Magazines					
Maps					
Models					
Murals					
Opaque projector					
Overhead projector					
Pictures					
Posters					
Records					
Tape recorder					
Other: _____					

When speaking to a group you must always be aware of these things:

1. Voice projection
2. Eye contact
3. Inflection

4. Proper grammar
5. Hand control
6. Posture

Name _____ Date _____

THINGS TO REMEMBER
WHEN PRESENTING YOUR PROJECT

Try to remember these rules when you are speaking before the group. Underline the ones you need to improve. On the lines at the bottom of this sheet, write any other rules and notes you feel you need as reminders.

1. Speak in complete sentences.
2. Use any new vocabulary words you may have learned, but be sure you can pronounce them and that you know what they mean.
3. Speak with a clear voice so that everyone can hear.
4. Look at your audience and speak to its members.
5. Stand aside when you are pointing out pictures, maps, charts, drawings, or diagrams.
6. Do not read long passages from your notes.
7. Know your material so that you sound like an informed person.
8. Be as calm as possible. Try to show that you have confidence in your work.
9. Do not chew gum when presenting.
10. Be ready to tell where you got your information.
11. Explain what your visual display shows, but don't read everything that is on it to your audience. Let the audience read it later.
12. Ask for questions from the class.
13. Be willing to admit that you don't know an answer if you really don't know.
14. Never make up an answer. You are expected to give only accurate information.
15. When your project is due to be presented, have it ready in final form—and on time! Do not come to class with empty hands and a list of excuses.

16. _____

_____

17. _____

_____

18. _____

_____

NOTES: _____

_____

_____

HOW TO USE THE DAILY LOG

Directions:

One of the most important requirements of an independent worker is an accurate record of each day's accomplishments. This is especially important for students who are just learning how to do research projects on their own. A Daily Log is helpful because every step of the project is recorded. This allows the teacher to check your progress without watching you work. The more conscientious you are about keeping a detailed, accurate log, the more likely you are to earn the right to become involved in even more independent projects.

To use the log on the next page, simply fill in the date and the time you started working on your project. Describe what you did as accurately as possible and record what was accomplished. Record the time when you are finished.

For example:

Oct. 14   10:45–11:25   Looked in 3 magazines for info. about earthquakes. Recorded facts on 10 notecards. Found 2 poster ideas.

DAILY LOG

Name: _____

Project Title: _____

Date Due: _____ Date Begun: _____ Date Completed: _____

DATE	TIME BEGUN	TIME ENDED	DESCRIPTION OF WORK

SKILLS CHART: SOCIAL STUDIES

#	Prerequisite Skills — Students must have command of these skills.
X	Primary Skills — Students will learn to use these skills; they are necessary to the project.
O	Secondary Skills — These skills may play an important role in certain cases.
*	Optional Skills — These skills may be emphasized but are not required.

	RESEARCH									WRITING						PLANNING				
	PREPARING BIBLIOGRAPHIES	COLLECTING DATA	INTERVIEWING	WRITING LETTERS	LIBRARY SKILLS	LISTENING	MAKING NOTECARDS	OBSERVING	SUMMARIZING	GRAMMAR	HANDWRITING	NEATNESS	PARAGRAPHS	SENTENCES	SPELLING	GROUP PLANNING	ORGANIZING	OUTLINING	SETTING OBJECTIVES	SELECTING TOPICS

SKILLS CHART: SOCIAL STUDIES

PROBLEM SOLVING						SELF-DISCIPLINE										SELF-EVALUATION				PRESENTATION								
BASIC MATHEMATICS SKILLS	DIVERGENT-CONVERGENT-EVALUATIVE THINKING	FOLLOWING & CHANGING PLANS	IDENTIFYING PROBLEMS	MEETING DEADLINES	WORKING w/LIMITED RESOURCES	ACCEPTING RESPONSIBILITY	CONCENTRATION	CONTROLLING BEHAVIOR	FOLLOWING PROJECT OUTLINES	INDIVIDUALIZED STUDY HABITS	PERSISTENCE	SHARING SPACE	TAKING CARE OF MATERIALS	TIME MANAGEMENT	WORKING WITH OTHERS	PERSONAL MOTIVATION	SELF-AWARENESS	SENSE OF "QUALITY"	SETTING PERSONAL GOALS	CREATIVE EXPRESSION	CREATING STRATEGIES	DIORAMA & MODEL BUILDING	DRAWING/SKETCHING/GRAPHING	POSTER MAKING	PUBLIC SPEAKING	SELF-CONFIDENCE	TEACHING OTHERS	WRITING